UNDERSTANDING ASTROLOGY

UNDERSTANDING ASTROLOGY

First steps in chart interpretation

by

Sasha Fenton

Thorsons
An Imprint of HarperCollins*Publishers*

Thorsons
An Imprint of HarperCollins*Publishers*
77–85 Fulham Palace Road,
Hammersmith, London W6 8JB
1160 Battery Street
San Francisco, California 94111–1213

Published by Aquarian, an imprint of Thorsons 1991
5 7 9 10 8 6 4

A catalogue record for this book
is available from the British Library

ISBN 1 85538 065 X

Printed and bound in Great Britain by
Caledonian International Book Manufacturing Ltd, Glasgow

CONTENTS

This book is dedicated to my friend, Frank Anderson, who took took on the onerous task of reading the proofs. There is no doubt that Arians have a real love of language and make the best proof-readers. They seem to be born with a natural ability to spell and to notice errors.

Thanks to Tony, Helen and Stuart Fenton who kept me supplied with cups of tea and didn't moan too much when I was too busy writing to remember to make dinner.

I would also like to thank Fred Baker of the South Wales Astrology Group (SWAG) for compiling all the charts and some of the tables.

INTRODUCTION

When I was learning astrology, I didn't know where to go for information. On mentioning my interest to an acquaintance, he put me in touch with a man who worked as a herbalist and used astrology to help him in his work. I phoned this herbalist and explained my predicament. He asked if I knew how to put a chart together and if I had any idea how to interpret it. When I said that I *could* do those things, he suggested, rather abruptly, that I do 500 charts 'because that is the only way to learn'. He then took his leave of me and put the phone down. I felt rather deflated and also embarrassed at having bothered such an unfriendly man, but I took his advice and it worked.

Nowadays, the student astrologer is spoilt for choice because there are so many books on the market and so many teaching organizations, that he or she may become confused. A visit to a bookshop which deals with these subjects and a chat to the people who work there might be useful, as would a visit to any of the New Age events and festivals which occur around the world. The Aquarian Press and other publishers send out booklists and brochures, so it is worthwhile getting yourself onto their mailing lists, particularly as this does not oblige you to buy anything. All astrological magazines advertise astrological schools and individuals who are willing to teach, along with mail-order booksellers and computer companies. Having found all this help, I suggest that you then do 500 charts ...

This book is not intended to be a complete course on astrology but it will be useful if you are teaching yourself or are involved in some kind of course. It may also help you if you want to do a bit of revision and take a fresh look at basic astrology.

What is a horoscope?

The word *horoscope* literally means 'a map of the hour'. A birthchart is, therefore, a map of the planets of the Solar system and the constellations of stars which appear to travel around the Earth. It is the precise location of these planets, along with the signs of the zodiac and their symbolic meanings, which describe a person's character and suggest areas of his personality which could grow and develop. The same principle can be applied to an enterprise, town, country or any event which an astrologer might wish to chart. The progress of the person, enterprise, etc., can subsequently be charted by the movement of the planets and constellations against the background of the original birthchart. The purpose of learning astrology, therefore, to understand the innate character of a person, place, situation or enterprise and to follow its development and the way it interacts with others over a period of time.

Fate and free will

I have met many people who think that their whole lives are mapped out for them and they only need to visit an astrologer to find the key. I don't believe this for a minute, although there are events which do indeed seem fated and which no amount of energy or effort seem to be able to prevent. We do seem to be fated in our choice of personality and character and perhaps this is handed down to us karmically as well as genetically before we are born. However, self-knowledge and an awareness of the movement of the planets and their meaning can do much to improve the way we cope with our lot in life.

Fred Baker and the hunt for Rowan Atkinson

The reasons for my choice of the example charts in this book are quite simple. I have been building up a small file of celebrity charts for some time and I have chosen to use here some from the sports and entertainment world as well as politics and a couple of Royals. In addition, I have chosen those whose charts did not have a large group of planets in a sign which is different from their Sun sign. For example, I rejected golfer Nick Faldo because, although he is a Sun in Cancer subject, he has so many planets in Leo that his Sun sign is overwhelmed. In some cases I was able to find the relevant data via the Astrological Association's David Fisher, who was formerly the guardian of a large celebrity database, but after that I ran out of ideas. It was at this point that the redoubtable Fred Baker came into his own.

I had chosen Fred to draw up the charts because I knew he would produce the clearest and best possible ones for reproduction in a book. I had forgotten that Fred is a Sun in Virgo subject and that all astrology books, including my own, tell us that Virgoans are a dab hand at research. Fred and his team of friends scoured the libraries and the various astrological databanks and found an amazing amount of information, but not even Fred's investigative powers could unearth anything on comedian Rowan Atkinson. He discovered that Rowan was born somewhere in the north or northern Midlands of England but could not find an exact place of birth and also no record of the time of his birth. Fred feels that Rowan probably has Virgo rising and I agree with his guess, it does feel right. However for the purpose of this book, Rowan's chart has been set at 0 degrees Aries rising. English cricketer Ian Botham's birth time also proved elusive as did the Queen Mother's, so we used Aries rising charts for these too. This is no bad thing because it gave the student a chance to look at a chart where the houses and angles are not wholly accurate as well as those which are.

As is usual in my books, I often resort to referring to 'he' and 'him' for ease of style. Astrological interpretations are non-sexist, of course, and apply equally to both sexes!

CHAPTER ONE

THE SUN THROUGH THE SIGNS

This first section of the book gives a brief introduction to the twelve Sun signs. Each Sun section ends with a celebrity's chart and a brief interpretation. You may find some of the technical parts of this interpretation difficult to follow at a first read. If you come back to them after reading the rest of the book, you should find the details much easier to understand.

♈ ## Aries

Ruled by Mars   **21 March — 20 April**

This is a masculine Fire sign which is Cardinal in nature and therefore the characteristics are those of courage, a love of adventure and travel, energy, enterprise, initiative and a determination to live life to the full.

Impulsive, enterprising, energetic, self-centred, generous, courageous, pioneering, highly-sexed ... I know, you've read all this before and it doesn't quite fit, does it? Now try this for size: home-loving, slow to change, a trifle mean, drawn to organized groups, interested in handicrafts and do-it-yourself schemes, spiritually-inclined and lacking in self-confidence. If this sounds suspiciously like many of your Arian friends and acquaintances, I wouldn't be surprised, because this is a complicated sign with many hidden folds in its personality.

Arian impulsiveness does exist, but only up to a point. For instance, if you ask your Arian friend to go out on a jaunt at short notice, he will be dressed and ready in an instant. If you ask for his help, it will be instantly and generously given. If you ask him to tackle something unfamiliar, he will have a go and probably make quite a good job of it. However, if you want him to give up his secure job, leave his family or change his life drastically, he will not do it! Being positive and optimistic by nature, the Arian will take an idea and run with it, but although his intuition is good his lack of attention to detail can catch him out, especially when someone else decides to take advantage of him. Arian competitiveness is expressed in everything he does: in sports, social life, business matters or by demonstrating his intellectual superiority. He may be a committee type of a pushy parent, but the need to compete never deserts the Arian although the game may change over the years. Arians want their own way and can be difficult when they don't get it.

Aries women are as competitive and demanding as the men. They are more suited to a career than to being a housewife but they can and do cope well with both situations at the same time. Traditional astrology suggests that Arians lack the capacity to follow through or to do a job thoroughly and in some cases this is true. However, they tend to stick with people and situations much longer than most, but when they do make up their minds to leave, they do so post-haste. In general, they are loving family people as long as they are allowed to pursue their career and hobby interests in peace. Many of them choose careers which allow them to spend part of their time away from home.

At work, Arians stay in a job for as long as possible, often rising to an executive position, but they sometimes change from jolly colleagues to unfeeling brutes when they reach the higher levels. This attitude stems from a lack of confidence and the underlying fear that they may not be good enough for the position which they have reached. Many Arians become teachers while others join large organizations such as the police, armed forces or civil service. They are drawn to jobs which help society while offering a well-defined ladder of advancement. Being bracketed by the two most creative and artistic signs of the zodiac — Pisces and Taurus — they often have a strongly artistic streak themselves and may have a hobby or a sideline which allows them to express this. I have met Arians who are very keen on music and others who are artists and craftsmen. However, I have come across those who, while they have a deep appreciation of arts and crafts on an intellectual level, are terrible bodgers when they try to do anything themselves.

In personal relationships, Aries men prefer strong women, while Aries women often take on motherly men. Arians are very faithful and supportive partners as long as there is mutual respect and the other aspects of their charts don't make them too restless. Some are never faithful, being imbued by the 'don't die wondering' syndrome but most, if they are lucky enough to find someone as strongly-sexed as they are and who understands their underlying lack of confidence, will stay put in a marriage. As children and often as adults too, they can be difficult to cope with, but their optimism, quick brain and sense of humour, plus their inability to hold a grudge, make them delightful companions. Their faults include selfishness and a peculiar mixture of frugality and overspending, as well as a quick temper and, in some cases, chronic untidiness. Arians can be very pushy parents who may bully their own children if they feel that they are not strong enough to stand up to them. They want their children to compete hard in everything that they do and to be winners. This is great if the children are Arian too but devastating if they are born under a more sensitive and doubting sign. Many Arians have a habit of walking out of the room in the middle of a conversation. But on the whole, those kind-hearted, loyal and caring people prefer to be happily involved with a group of friends and a loving family than to cause friction or be destructive in any way.

Jeffrey Archer   **15 April 1940**

Novelist Jeffrey Archer has his Sun and Jupiter in Aries in the strong and angular tenth house, so he is imbued with typical Arian

BIRTH CHART

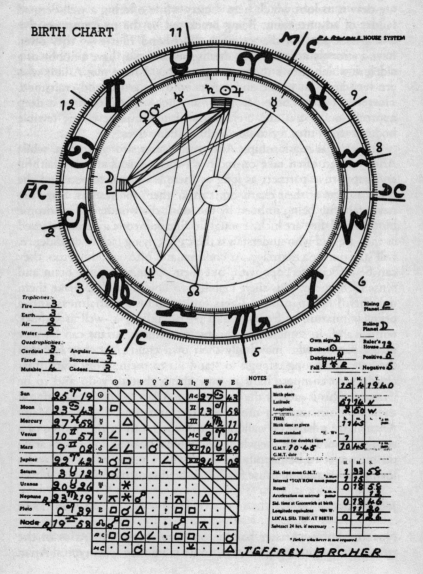

PARSONS HOUSE SYSTEM

JEFFREY ARCHER

14

ambition, energy and enterprise. He has tried to be a part of large organizations from time to time but seems to be luckier and better off doing his own thing. There are many interesting features on his chart; for example, Jeffrey's Pluto and Moon, which are both close to the ascendant, make him reach out towards the public for his living and also give him a quite genuine urge to change things for the better. Arians are usually idealistic although they may not always appear that way to others. The opposition between Mercury which is on his midheaven to Neptune which is down by the nadir are responsible for his rich imagination but also for the peculiar mysteries which surround him from time to time. Saturn in the 10th house in Taurus which is in square aspect to his Pluto in the 1st, gives him the ability to complete creative or artistic tasks and to present them to the public. However, this situation is also responsible for the public acclaim and the public notoriety which have been the pattern of his life.

 # Taurus

Ruled by Venus   **21 April — 21 May**

This is a feminine Earth sign which is Fixed in nature. Therefore the characteristics are of nurturing, patience, thoroughness, tenacity, obstinacy and reliability.

Astrology books often accuse Taureans of being plodding, boring and rather insensitive people who are only interested in food and money. My own experience of Taureans is that they are intensely loyal to their families and friends, while having a number of deep interests and a great sense of humour. This is an intensely creative sign which leads many of its subjects into artistic careers. Those who don't work in an artistic field have hobbies or interests which allow them to express their artistry. Food and drink certainly does interest many Taureans, leading many of them into careers in the food and drink industry or into hobbies such as cake decorating or wine tasting. However, many are interested in history, while many others are very keen musicians and dancers. Most are very dextrous, making excellent craftsmen who are never clumsy or rash in their execution of a task. I have even come across one or two who are involved in astrology but, on the whole, Taureans are apt to be uncomfortable with esoteric subjects. Being a Fixed Earth sign, Taureans prefer to deal with the things they can see, touch, hear, smell and taste. Some Taureans use their strength and determination to succeed in business and they are helped in this by their charming, relaxed manner and pleasant appearance.

A few Taureans are highly eccentric, choosing to wear strange clothes and to follow an adventurous way of life, but behind this eccentricity hides a person who works hard and is reliable in family and relationship matters. Most Taureans are highly conscious of their image and hate to behave in an embarrassing manner or to look ridiculous. Taureans have suburban standards, having a need for a decent home, a steady partner, children and, above all, a garden. They need to put down roots, in every sense of the word and many of them are excellent builders and house decorators. This doesn't preclude the Taurean from having an extra-marital affair or two if he or she feels like it, but they rarely leave the happy home to live with a lover. Such people maintain the status quo and do not easily give up on jobs, people or their beliefs. When faced with uncertainty, they become very nervy and upset, but they cope better than most when forced to change. These people have courage and endurance and the ability to see things through. One form of change that many of them do enjoy is travel, preferably in five-star luxury. However, they need to know that their home is waiting for their return. The Taurean needs to know where his loved ones are and would feel very unhappy living with an unpredictable type who disappears for hours on end without telling anyone where he or she is going.

Taureans thoroughly enjoy lovemaking. Their patience and sensuality ensures that they give as much pleasure as they receive and they don't treat making love as a race or a competitive sport; they simply enjoy it for what it is. Taurean likes and dislikes are strong and their ideas are fixed. They are practical, sensible and patient with a deep need for security of all kinds. They have a reputation for being money-minded and tight-fisted and this is true in many cases. While they are generous to their families and those who matter to them, they don't hand out goodies to all and sundry. They are not notable givers of charity. Taureans hate waste and can buy the makings of a dinner party with such accuracy that nothing is left over. Taurean standards are high, they prefer to tell the truth and to deal fairly. As lovers, they are sincere and loyal. They make admirable marriage partners and excellent parents but, unless there is something lighter on their birthcharts, they can lack imagination and be too ready to fall into a rut. Their own childhood is usually adequate in a practical sense but they are often led to feel that they don't measure up and will never count for anything. Taureans rarely shine at school or anywhere else while young and can all too easily be used as cheap labour around the home whilst being undervalued as personalities.

Many Taureans are the salt of the earth while others, particularly older men of the sign, become impossible to live with later in life. These Venus-ruled people can be very, very lazy in relationships once the initial sexual frisson has worn off.

Maureen Lipman   **10 May 1946**

If actress Maureen Lipman doesn't seem to be the usual overweight Taurus clerk beloved of most astrology books, the fact that none of her planets except the Sun are actually in Taurus may have something to do with it. However, Fred Astaire was also a Taurean and he didn't have much weight to spare either. Maureen's dedication to her craft and her family are typically Taurean as is her wonderful sense of humour. She is artistically gifted in many different directions and can turn her hand to almost anything. Her conjunction of Venus and Uranus in Gemini probably has something to do with this. All Earth sign people tend to look better as they get older and Maureen is no exception. Like many Taureans, she has an equivocal relationship with her mother and mixed feelings about her childhood, acknowledging the benefits that accrued while admitting that it could have been a lot better. Neptune in conjunction with Mars in Leo allows her to make solid

BIRTH CHART

PLACIDUS HOUSE SYSTEM

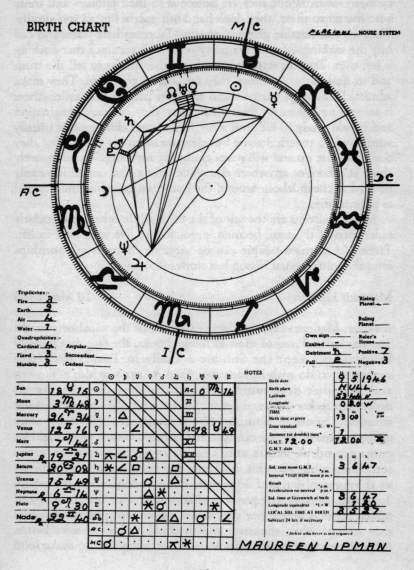

Triplicities:-	
Fire	3
Earth	3
Air	4
Water	7

Quadruplicities:-			
Cardinal	4	Angular	
Fixed	3	Succedent	
Mutable	3	Cadent	

Rising Planet	—
Ruling Planet	—

Own sign	—	Ruler's House	—
Exalted	—		
Detriment	♄	Positive	7
Fall	♇	Negative	3

	⊙	☽	☿	♀	♂	♃	♄	♅	♆	♇		
Sun	18 ♉ 15	⊙									AC	0 ♍ 16
Moon	3 ♏ 49	☽									II	
Mercury	26 ♈ 34	☿	·	△							III	
Venus	12 ♊ 16	♀	·	·	∠						MC	28 ♉ 49
Mars	7 ♋ 41	♂	·								XI	
Jupiter ℞	19 ♍ 21	♃	⊼	∠	♂	△					XII	
Saturn	20 ♋ 08	♄	✳	∠	□	·	□					
Uranus	15 ♊ 49	♅	·	·	△	△	△	·				
Neptune	6 ♎ 14	♆	·		△	△	✳	✳	·			
Pluto	9 ♌ 30	♇	·		✳	△	·	✳	·	✳		
Node ℞	22 ♊ 40	☊	·	✳	·	△	△	·	♂	·	∠	
		AC		♂ △								
		MC			·	⊼	✳	·				

NOTES

	H.	M.	Y.
Birth date	9	5	1946
Birth place	HULL		
Latitude	53 44 N		
Longitude	0 20 W		
TIME	H.	M.	
Birth time as given	73	00	p.m.
Zone standard *E·W*	7		
Summer (or double) time*			
G.M.T. 12.00	12	00	⚡
G.M.T. date			
	H.	M.	S.
Sid. time noon G.M.T.	3	6	47
Interval *TO FROM noon p.m.*			
Result *a.m.* *p.m.*			
Acceleration on interval p.m.			
Sid. time at Greenwich at birth	3	6	47
Longitude equivalent *E·W*		1	20
LOCAL SID. TIME AT BIRTH	3	5	27
Subtract 24 hrs if necessary			

* Delete whichever is not required

MAUREEN LIPMAN

use of her imagination and creative talents but it might make her moody and irritable at times. I guess that her Taurean Sun keeps her to a routine of work, exercise and family life which should make her feel comfortable and secure.

♊ Gemini

Ruled by Mercury   **21 May — 21 June**

Gemini is a masculine sign which is Mutable in character. Therefore the characteristics are adventurous, outgoing, restless and assertive but adaptable.

This is a much misunderstood sign. Gemini subjects are often being accused of shallowness, shortage of intellect, inability to stick to anything or anyone, being great fun at a party, but totally unreliable. *Not true!* Geminis are ambitious and hard working, reliable and capable while they have their mind on the job. If they lose interest in something it becomes history, and Geminis are not attracted to history. These people need plenty of variety in their lives and in their work because an unchanging routine bores them; however they can cope with more pressure than most and can do five jobs at once. Geminis need to communicate and will often do so for a living. Their idea of hell would be to be taken hostage and kept in solitary confinement.

Oddly enough, Geminis stick to their relationships, often remaining close to their parents, children and partners throughout their lives. However, I wouldn't like to guarantee their fidelity. The problem here is the famed Gemini curiosity. They are drawn to interesting people and may not think too much about their family obligations while the attraction lasts, but they rarely go as far as to leave a partner if they can help it. Don't expect them to sacrifice themselves for suffering humanity because Geminis are conscious of the fact that they are not physically strong and need to conserve their energies for themselves and those they love. These talented people can do practically anything they put their mind to, as long as it isn't boring. They enjoy travel, sports and hobbies and can often turn a hobby into a successful part-time job. Geminis are more sensible, capable and hard-working than they are given credit for but they do have a tendency to be selfish and indifferent to the needs of others. An ambitious Gemini will charge down his chosen pathway with little regard for the needs of others. The gentler, more easy-going type is good company, if a little inclined to whine at time. Most Geminis are great flirts but like the other two Air signs, may be slow to make a full commitment to a relationship. Gemini is known to be a clever sign and yet these subjects may not be very well read, preferring to pick up their information from other people or from the television or an adult education class. Some are accused of knowing a little about a lot — surely better than the specialist who knows practically everything about very little? — but most of these subjects are very keen on education and have a deep and abiding knowledge of at least one subject. Geminis can be very cheeky, using their charms and sense of humour to get away with far more than the more serious zodiac types can.

Geminis seem to miss out on the joys of childhood, often feeling like a square peg in a round hole. I call this the sign of the orphan, (although true orphans are more likely to have Gemini as a rising sign rather than as a Sun sign). In marriage, Geminis are not too bad — they can stray, of course, but many of them don't. They need something more than a relationship alone to stimulate them and usually pour their heart and soul into a career. If you have a Gemini partner and want to see plenty of him, start up a business together. In a love relationship, they are surprisingly constant and their famed ability to flirt is unlikely to lead them into too much trouble. Geminis are not attracted to housework. They like to live in nice surroundings, but wiping down paintwork and cleaning out the fridge hold no pleasures for them at all. Gemini women often marry domesticated men who are happy to take on these chores for them. Others employ a cleaner and, because they are reasonable employers, they keep their staff for years. Unless a Gemini subject has a couple of planets in nearby Cancer and Leo, he won't be a brilliant parent. There are a number of reasons for this. Firstly, parenthood takes more patience and a higher boredom threshold than the average Gemini can muster. Secondly, Geminis of both sexes tend to be highly involved with careers and are frequently tired and preoccupied when they get home. Thirdly, these subjects may be pushy and competitive with regard to their children and they may not be willing to see them as human beings but only as achievement machines which are designed to enhance the status of the parents. The Gemini's inability to relate to his parents and the failure of those parents to love the Gemini in his own right may make it difficult for him to understand the needs of his own children. Geminis are not alone in this, for all the Air signs are somewhat lacking as parents.

One thing Geminis are good at is dealing with money. They make excellent accountants and bankers and have a speed and intuition in business matters which makes other people wonder. They love to travel and often do so in connection with their work. They are fascinated by the world of astrology and the esoteric and attend every psychic festival in large numbers. They tend to be good-looking people who have a terrific sense of humour and a realistic approach to life. They don't put on airs and their manners are impeccable. They want the best for themselves and their families and are prepared to work hard for it.

Steffi Graf   **14 June 1969**

The sign of Gemini rules the hands, arms, shoulders and lungs. It is also associated with speed of action, dexterity and sportsmanship, so it is not surprising that top tennis player Steffi Graf is a Sun in Gemini subject. Her Sun, Moon and Mercury are all in the twelfth house which would make her an excellent clairvoyant palmist in addition to being a top sportswoman! If you have read Michael Gauquelin's books about astrology and careers, you will remember that planets in the twelfth house are great indicators of success. According to Monsieur Gauquelin's theories, a top sportsman or woman needs to have Mars in one of the cadent houses, and when we look at her chart, we see that Steffi's Mars is perfectly placed in the 6th house. Mars in the 6th suggests great energy being put into work, but the accompanying Neptune could bring inspiration but

BIRTH CHART

PLACIDUS HOUSE SYSTEM

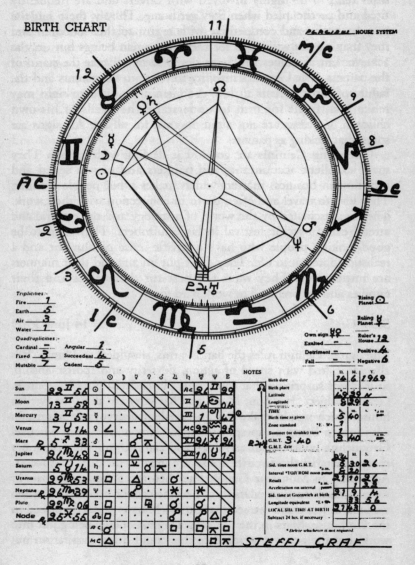

Triplicities:-

Fire **1**
Earth **5**
Air **3**
Water **1**

Quadruplicities:-

Cardinal **—**   Angular **2**
Fixed **3**   Succeedent **4**
Mutable **7**   Cadent **4**

Rising Planet ☉
Ruling Planet ☿

Own sign ♀   Ruler's House **12**
Exalted **—**   Positive **4**
Detriment **—**   Negative **6**
Fall **—**

	☉	☽	☿	♀	♂	♃	♄	♅	♆	♇		NOTES		D.	M.	Y.
Sun	22 ♊ 56	☉									AC	24 ♊ 99	Birth date	16	6	1969
Moon	13 ♊ 58	☽	·									14 ♊ 06	Birth place			
Mercury	3 ♊ 53	☿	·	·							♏	1 ♏ 47	Latitude		48 50	N
													Longitude		8 29	E
Venus	7 ♉ 14	♀	∠								MC	23 ♒ 95	**TIME**	H.	M.	
													Birth time as given	5	40	ᴬ·ᴹ·
Mars	R 5 ♑ 33	♂	·		□	⊼					XI	16 ♓ 96	Zone standard *E. W*	1		
													Summer (or double) time*	1		
Jupiter	26 ♏ 48	♃	□	·	·	·					XII	10 ♈ 75	G.M.T.	3	40	ᴬ·ᴹ·
Saturn	5 ♉ 14	♄	·	⊼	□	♂	⊼				R ♃		G.M.T. date			
Uranus	99 ♈ 53	♅	·	·	△	·	♂							D.	M.	Y.
													Sid. time noon G.M.T.	5	30	26
Neptune	26 ♏ 39	♆	·	♂	·	·	✶	·					Interval *TO/FROM noon	3	10	26
													Result	21	70	ᴾ·ᴹ·
Pluto	22 ♏ 06	♇	□	·	□	□	♂	♂					Acceleration on interval			M.
													Sid. time at Greenwich at birth	21	9	ᴬ·ᴹ·
Node	R 25 ♓ 56	☊	□	·		·	△	△	△				Longitude equivalent *E. *W		33	56
													LOCAL SID. TIME AT BIRTH	21	43	0
											AC	♂	Subtract 24 hrs. if necessary			
											MC	△				

Delete whichever is not required.

STEFFI GRAF

also the feeling that from time to time everything is slipping a
from her.

Saturn in the 11th house in Taurus suggests that Steffi has the
patience and tenacity to learn as she goes through life and will never
stop training and studying her craft. Venus close to Saturn in the
11th in Taurus suggests influential and wealthy acquaintances but
also a great social life with some really wonderful female friends.
Sagittarius on the cusp of the 7th indicates a need for freedom in
relationships or the need to marry someone from a traditional
religious or cultural background. Notice the powerful stellium in
Virgo in the 4th and 5th houses. Virgo suggests discipline and
dedication to a line of work which is essentially a game. Games are
a 5th house activity. Did she have a childhood, or was she hatched
full-blown into adulthood the minute she picked up a tennis
racquet? With the Sun, Moon and ascendant in the cold, sterile
orphan's sign of Gemini, she must have felt at time as if she didn't
know what it was to be childish and carefree. If that were not
enough, three planets in Virgo would have made her upbringing a
catalogue of almost military-style discipline. She is ambitious on
her own behalf, however, so her parents and trainers have found her
to be a willing horse — most of the time at least.

♋ Cancer

Ruled by the Moon   **22 June — 23 July**

Cancer is a feminine sign which is Cardinal and Watery in nature.
This means that Cancerians seek to nurture and protect but in a
surprisingly assertive manner and are not afraid of taking the
initiative on behalf of those they love.

Cancerians look soft but are stubborn and surprisingly tough.
They are interested in people and have a kindly sympathetic nature.
Their ability to really listen to what others have to say makes them
excellent at dealing with the public. These people have a good deal
of intuition which, when allied to their shrewd and careful nature,

can make them extremely successful in any field in which they choose to operate. They have the ability to defuse a situation and to cope with the moods of others without becoming unduly involved themselves, which makes them excellent teachers, counsellors and small business owners. They are usually sensible, reasonable and hard-working, but oddly enough rarely lucky in matters of money. They make enough to keep going but, unless there is some other strong influence on their charts, they tend to step off the ladder before they reach the bit which leads to real wealth. They seem to lack adaptability and they fear change. They also fear being upset or getting in touch with their emotions. They have a strong sense of privacy and, although superficially friendly, tend to keep most people at arms' length until they know them very well.

Many Cancerians devote themselves to their families and are very good to those relatives who need their help and support. They need a home base and to have their families within hailing distance, but they love to take trips away from home and can be frequent travellers. They are not too fond of their own company, preferring to work and live among a sympathetic group of people. They are surprisingly political and often hold office in some kind of club or society, sometimes being more successful in this area than in their careers. They are wonderful allies but can be implacable and quite dangerous enemies.

Cancerians tend to look backwards rather than forwards and feel safe with places and objects which are familiar to them. They don't move house readily and prefer to stay in the same job or business over a period of years. They can put up with quite difficult circumstances at work but need peace and harmony in their homes. Many Cancerians are interested in history, especially military history, and spend some part of their spare time in historical or militaristic organizations. Oddly enough, these peace-loving and gentle people are often experts on weapons and war machinery. Many collect antiques, coins, books or junk. This instinct to hoard makes them great savers of money and they love to pick up a bargain. A few Cancerians are dishonest because they can't seem to see the dividing line between what is theirs and what belongs to somebody else, although most are extremely honest.

Cancer is a very domestic sign and its subject are usually good home-makers. A Cancerian home is not normally pin-neat, but neither is it a pit of medieval squalor. It is a comfortable place, with ageing furniture and an appetising smell emanating from the kitchen. Cancerians of both sexes can be very creative cooks. They enjoy eating but prefer to stick to plain, old-fashioned food as they tend to have sensitive stomachs. Cancerians don't seem to be great drinkers, possibly due to that sensitive tummy, but they do enjoy an occasional glass of good wine. Many Cancerians like to grow food for themselves in a garden or greenhouse and are also fond of flowers. Some are great animal lovers who choose to keep a number of pets or even work with animals, while others hate and fear animals and don't want them anywhere near them.

Cancerian faults are those of clannishness and suspicion of outsiders. They are extremely sensitive and will avoid people who have the power to hurt them. Partners of these subjects complain that they can become crotchety for no apparent reason and, having got themselves into an unpleasant frame of mind, they don't know how to get themselves out of it again. Their surface charm and friendliness is so convincing that one has to live with them to really know what they can be like, and people outside the family may find it hard to believe that they can be downright bloody. If you live with or work with a Cancerian you must stand up to them because they respect strength. Cancerians are worriers, they can work themselves up over the most trivial things and also try to cross every hurdle before meeting it. Some Cancerians become more laid-back later in life, but it usually takes a conscious effort on their behalf.

Cancerians tend to cling to those whom they love, especially their children. Cancer subjects are themselves slow to grow up and, if they get on well with their parents, may not leave home and set up their own families until quite late. They expect their children to remain close to them throughout life. Once committed to a relationship, Cancerians prefer to stick to their chosen partner and will put up with quite a difficult lifestyle if necessary. If they divorce, they tend to look for a new partner and they don't mind taking on someone who has a large family of their own to look after. Many Cancerians like being married to a more outgoing and opportunistic partner because then they can enjoy the thrills and pleasures of high-level successes and failures at second hand. They are wonderfully supportive to a partner who takes the risks in life for them, so to speak. Cancerians love novelty and a break from their usual routine. Most of them are great travellers and are quite prepared to go anywhere at the drop of a hat. Traditionally Cancerians are supposed to love the sea but I have discovered that they love any kind of open space.

Barbara Cartland   9 July 1901

Dame Barbara Cartland grew up in a happy family and was a good-looking and outgoing girl. She obviously put a lot into being a mother which is shown by the success of her children. She discovered an ability to write romantic fiction and has kept herself happily occupied in this for years. Like many Cancerians, she works from home with a well-organized staff around to help her.

Barbara Cartland's Sun, Mercury and imaginative Neptune in her 3rd house of communications are responsible for her writing ability, while her Venus in the 4th house keeps her in or near her home. Her ascendant is in the outgoing and 'me first' sign of Aries, as is the Moon which is her rising planet. She is obviously very sensitive but has turned to her ability to tap into the sensitivity of others in order to make a living. Her books are all about feelings and the need for love, and many of them have historical themes, which is all typically Cancerian. Her outer manner is quite outrageous and, despite all her efforts at femininity, surprisingly masculine due to that thrusting, energetic and masculine Aries influence on her ascendant and her Moon. Her midheaven is in the patient, ambitious and capable sign of Capricorn which tells us something about her tenacity — and her longevity. It is bracketed by fortunate Jupiter which is comfortable in its own house (the 9th) and the hard-working and craftmanlike Saturn in the 10th. Saturn in the tenth indicates great public success and acclaim, which is often achieved quite late in life. It can also denote a tremendous public fall from grace but this, fortunately, hasn't happened.

BIRTH CHART

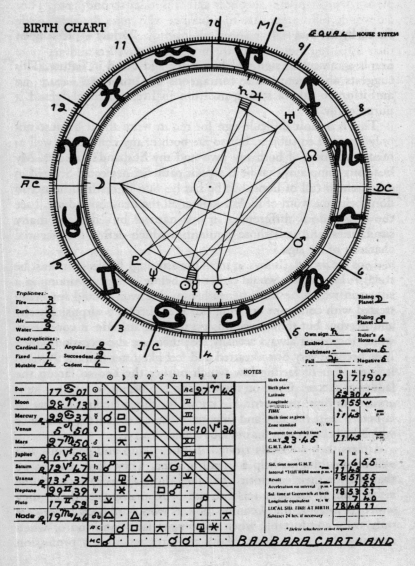

♌ Leo

Ruled by the Sun   **23 July — 23 August**

Leo is a masculine sign which is Fiery and Fixed in nature. This suggests an adventurous, courageous but stubborn nature, an ambition to take a strong position in life and then defend it purposefully.

This is a most difficult sign for me to write about because not only am I a Leo subject, but so are both of my children as well as many members of both my own and my husband's families. My husband complains that he is a poor pathetic, neglected Scorpio in a household full of lions, but he has his Sun in his fifth house, so don't believe a word of it! As I look at all the Leos around me, I see the tremendous differences in our natures but also the many similarities, and it is those similarities which define the essential character of the sign.

Leos are proud. (It says so in all the astrology books so it must be true!) A Leo subject would rather die before living or working in a situation which he finds beneath him. He won't stand for being treated with contempt or being ridiculed. Leos are surprisingly shy and nervous but they cover this up with an attitude of confidence which they don't always actually feel; there are also occasions when Leos become very downhearted and feel like utter failures. Perhaps it is the fear of feeling low which pushes the Leo so far up the ladder of success. Once on his way, the Leo begins to feel that he is entitled to royal treatment. He knows (or thinks he knows) that he is better than the rest and expects to be accorded the deference which he believes that his obvious talents deserve.

Unless they are badly treated, Leos are kind and generous and will do anything to help a friend in need. They don't need to be thanked for their generosity, but they don't appreciate ingratitude either and, if someone seeks to use or to manipulate them, they won't get away with it. Leonine subjects work hard because they are only truly comfortable when in a supervisory position or when running their own show. Many are attracted to any profession which provides a sport of glamour and they will work hard at anything they enjoy without caring too much about their rate of pay. However, they do tend to go for the jobs which bring in money, partly because they are big spenders but also because a high salary implies a high status. Leos are either absolutely honest, reliable, decent and honourable or complete scoundrels. Leos can also be competitive and extremely hard in business, showing little mercy for those whom they overtake in their race for the top. This is somewhat strange, because in general these natives would far rather help someone up the ladder than stand in their way. Some Leos are permanently in debt and don't consider this a problem while others hate owing even one penny to another. Both extremes reflect a need to be in control of their own lives and not to be bothered by the opinions of others. Appearances are important to Leos, they need a nice home, a good car, beautiful clothes and quality in everything. Leos are snobs, being fussy about their choice of friends, the school their children attend, their holiday destination and even the shops they use. A coach full of revellers chanting 'earwig-o, earwig-o' on their holidays in August is their idea of hell!

Leo faults include impatience and a tendency to overdramatize problems. They become very irritable and difficult when under pressure and can panic when things go inexplicably wrong. They also have a hot temper. However, none of this lasts for long. If something makes Leonine subjects feel panicky and out of control, they quickly take hold of themselves and handle the situation with more courage and lateral thinking than the rest of the zodiac put together. Depression, bad temper or unhappiness soon pass because these subjects would far rather be happy and good-natured than otherwise. Leos can be pompous, arrogant and overbearing but this may be a reaction to pressure than a normal form of behaviour.

Leos excel as family members, being extremely fond of their children and good to their parents. They are sensitive to the needs of others, especially those who are close to them. They want to help their loved ones and hate to see them unhappy. However, as parents this does not imply that they are soft. Their ideas are quite old-fashioned and they believe that children should learn to behave properly and to treat adults with due respect. Leos believe strongly in education, and will go to great lengths to see that their children receive the best that money can buy. Leo mothers are not over-maternal. They need to work and to have interests of their own and are rapidly bored by a lifestyle which offers little other than housework and child-minding. Leos are old-fashioned in their attitude to relationships as well. Once they decide to marry, they will stick to the arrangement through thick and thin, only leaving if the situation becomes really impossible. They hate to lose touch with their children. If happy, a Leo will be a faithful and trustworthy partner, but if something goes wrong he may look for love outside the marriage while still living with and looking after his partner.

Leo hobbies and interests include anything which offers adventure and a touch of glamour. Most enjoy travel, preferably in five-star comfort, while others love sports and adventure. Many Leos work with young people but all will avoid anything which involves being dirty, cold, uncomfortable or looking daft. They are good hosts and also appreciative guests but they don't like to overstay their welcome, preferring to make short visits, returning home while everyone is still happy with each other. They also like snoozing on the sofa.

The Queen Mother   4 August 1900

The Queen Mother's birth is something of a mystery. The latest information which I have is that she was born in London, possibly on a moving vehicle! All that we know for certain is the date of birth and the now reasonable certainty that she was born in London. To have achieved such longevity and remain in such a good state of health, she would need a reasonable helping of both Capricorn and Gemini on her chart. It is well known that Capricorn is associated with old age but you may be a little surprised by my comments about Gemini. The fact is that I have noticed time and time again that late Taurus and early Gemini seems to be associated with people who live for a long time. Furthermore, these people continue working long after anyone else

BIRTH CHART

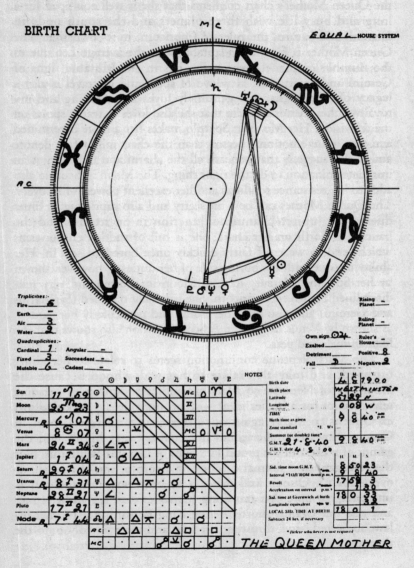

EQUAL HOUSE SYSTEM

THE QUEEN MOTHER

would have sank gratefully into the nearest bathchair. One look at the Queen Mother's chart confirms that she is well equipped for a long and busy life with three planets and the south node in Gemini, and Saturn, the ruler of Capricorn, in its own sign. The Queen Mother is far more adaptable than the average Leo due to the number of planets which she has in the Mutable signs of Gemini and Sagittarius. Her love of sport and of travel is also a legacy of these signs. She genuinely loves horse-racing and my royal-watcher friends confirm that she also loves to watch sports on the television. Her Moon in Scorpio makes her a more determined and also more emotional person than the chart might first denote and it also suggests that beneath all the charm and flexibility is an iron determination to do the right thing. The Moon in Scorpio also adds to her resistance to illness and her excellent powers of recovery. The Queen Mother can be a bit scatty and also capricious at times due to the Jupiter/Uranus conjunction in Sagittarius and the paucity of Earth on her chart. She is full of sudden enthusiasms which tend to wear off fairly quickly once boredom sets in. Her ability to cope with the boring side of her duties is, however, shown by her Sun and Mercury in Leo, Moon in Scorpio and very self-disciplined Saturn in Capricorn. She is widely travelled (Sagittarius and Gemini) and also loves her home and particularly her garden, as shown by Venus in Cancer. A Scorpio Moon also shows that she likes animals and pets.

The Mars/Neptune conjunction seems to relate to her ailing husband, and may also relate to her widowhood because the proximity of Neptune to Mars can indicate sacrifice of personal relationships for a higher ideal — I am not sure if protocol allows ex-Queens to marry again once their husbands die. Venus in Cancer shows that she values her country very highly and the gamut of planets in the proud Fire signs of Leo and Sagittarius, plus that arrogant and dramatic Moon in Scorpio, shows that she is every inch a Queen and expects to be treated as such. It is interesting to note that transiting Jupiter crossed her natal Jupiter and also her Uranus shortly before King Edward, her brother-in-law, abdicated, thus thrusting her husband unexpectedly onto the throne.

♍ Virgo

Ruled by Mercury   **24 August — 23 September**

Virgo is feminine, Mutable and Earthy in nature. This makes it practical, nurturing, flexible and a strange mixture of activity and passivity.

Virgo is a strangely misunderstood sign. These subjects are depicted as being modest, hard-working, gentle and dull, preferring a subordinate role and running away from anything which looks like being fun. Yet this sign is ruled by Mercury which is anything but dull and it is an Earth sign which implies a strongly sensual nature. Many Virgos are very independent and even somewhat eccentric. Virgoans have very high standards; they expect themselves to be perfect and can also expect perfection of others. It is not surprising that some of them find life disappointing at times. They are their own harshest critics and can also be abrupt and critical in their dealings with others. However, their shyness, natural good manners and their desire not to cause distress to others usually curbs this impulse to a great extent. They work very hard, do things quickly and are excellent at details. They are also amazingly self-disciplined. Virgoans, along with their Capricorn cousins, are the craftsmen of the zodiac. They are rarely lazy and hate to be accused of inefficiency, They can appear a bit cool and unemotional but this is a shield behind which they hide because they are sensitive and easily embarrassed. Virgoans are loyal and devoted but they won't be taken for granted and are quick to spot those who seek to use or abuse them. They are helpful, kind and dutiful and they offer the very best in friendship but their tendency to worry about nothing can be irritating. They abhor cruelty and are so soft-hearted that they cannot even bear to hear about cruel acts. They are kind to animals, and may, indeed, prefer them to human beings, although Virgoans often have a soft spot for the elderly. They have a natural talent for medical matters and don't mind nursing a sick family member.

Virgoans are successful in any career which requires attention to detail. They are excellent communicators and can happily cope with many careers which are usually attributed to the sign of Gemini, such as journalism and telecommunications work. They can be too fussy and demanding for some people's tastes and can also be so concerned with perfection that they sometimes can't see the wood for the trees! Virgoans are happier as team members or assistants to more powerful personalities, but they do need to be appreciated. They are not comfortable in positions of authority, because they are too shy and awkward to be able to give orders. They may cover up for this by being difficult or sarcastic when they inadvertently find themselves in positions of power. They prefer to work with their intellect, by solving problems, grappling with tricky machinery or specializing in some aspect of science or medicine.

Most Virgoans are health conscious and many are fussy about food. Quite a number are vegetarians while others would prefer not to eat at all, if that were possible. Some Virgoans smoke — but compensate for the health hazard by worrying and feeling guilty about it. Some are hypochondriacs or anxiety-ridden neurotics, although most are perfectly sensible. One very popular outlet for Virgoans is acting, because this allows them to set aside their diffidence and put on a mask. Another outlet is sport which allows them to compete with others in a permissible and gentlemanly or ladylike manner. Most are good drivers; remember their ruling planet, Mercury.

In relationships, Virgoans are steadfast and loyal, fond of their families and happy to show their love in practical ways. They may be embarrassed by displays of open affection, especially in front of others, but in private they are very loving. This is an Earth sign so Virgoans are surprisingly sensual and sexual but refined and delicate in their approach. The only real problem in a close relationship is their tendency to criticize. Their parents criticized them and they may have been programmed to think that criticism is a way of showing love. Virgoans are dutiful and caring partners, they are fair and reasonable and more honest than most. They are easily hurt and deflated, therefore they tend to attach themselves to strong partners who can cherish them and shield them from the big wide world. Unfortunately, this doesn't always work out and they can find themselves attached to users or losers. Another potential problem in relationships is that they can be too demanding in terms of cleanliness and standards of housekeeping. They can be too rigid and unable to relax and have a good laugh. Fortunately this improves with age and is helped because Virgoans are relatively unselfish.

Virgo hobbies can range from creative ones such as painting, cookery and sewing to group interests such as belonging to masonic and religious organizations. They also like to be of service to the community and many are keen on sports and acting. Virgoans enjoy the company of a very few old and trusted friends, although many of them are at their happiest when working.

Pete Murray   **19 September 1925**

Pete is an actor, sportsman and very well-known British radio and television presenter. Middle-aged people will remember him hosting the *Six-Five Special* show which was the first pop music programme on television. I work with Pete regularly on London Talkback Radio and know him to be totally professional, highly competent and absolutely reliable in his work. He is a shy man who is incredibly kind and very soft-hearted. He worries about his elderly mother and takes care of everyone around him. He is universally known as a real 'sweetie' although, like all Virgoans, he can be irritable and awkward at times. Pete is a typical Virgo being shy, modest and hard-working. He is interested in all things psychic and very encouraging to those of us who work in the field. He is tolerant and caring and hates narrow-minded people who try to thrust their views down the throats of others. He can't stand to hear about cruelty and suffering of any kind. It is no surprise to find, therefore, that his ascendant is Sagittarius.

His rise to fame and fortune is not surprising when one considers his Libran midheaven which is closely bracketed by his Sun in Virgo and Moon in Libra with Mars alongside the Sun. His Sun/Mars conjunction suggests a strong drive to achieve and succeed, allied to a powerful temper. He may have grown out of

BIRTH CHART

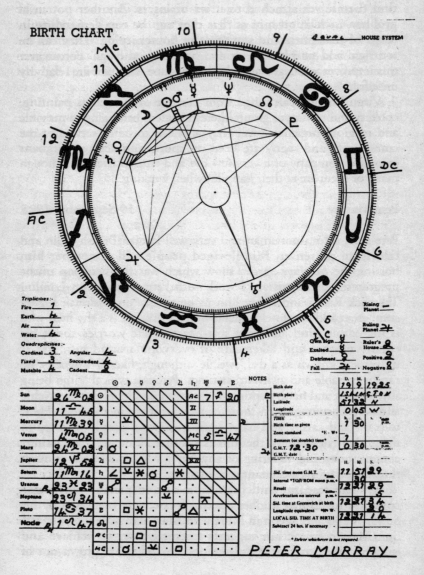

Equal HOUSE SYSTEM

Triplicities:-
Fire	1		
Earth	4		
Air	1		
Water	4		

Quadruplicities:-
Cardinal	3	Angular	4
Fixed	3	Succeedent	2
Mutable	4	Cadent	2

Rising Planet —
Ruling Planet 24

Own Sign	4	
Exalted	4	Ruler's House	8
Detriment	9	Positive	8
Fall	24	Negative	8

	⊙	☽	☿	♀	♂	♃	♄	♅	♆	♇		NOTES		D.	M.	Y.
Sun	26 ♏ 03	⊙									AC 7 ♐ 20	Birth date		19	9	1925
Moon	11 ♎ 45	☽	·								II	Birth place		ISLINGTON		
Mercury	11 ♏ 39	☿	✓	·							III	Latitude		51	32	N
Venus	4 ♏ 05	♀	·	·	·						MC 5 ♎ 47	Longitude		0	05	W
												TIME		H.	M.	
Mars	24 ♑ 03	♂	♂	·	·	·					XI	Birth time as given		1	30	P.M.
Jupiter	12 ♑ 58	♃	·	□	△	·	·				XII	Zone standard *E - W*				
Saturn	11 ♏ 16	♄	✓	✓	□	♂	·	✳				Summer (or double) time*		1		
Uranus	23 ♓ 23	♅	□	·	·	·	♂	·				G.M.T. 12·30		0	30	
Neptune	23 ♌ 34	♆	·	·	·	✓	·	·	✓		✗	G.M.T. date				
Pluto	14 ♋ 37	♇	□	✳	·	·	♂	△	·					H.	M.	S.
Node	1 ♌ 47 ℞	☊	·	·	·	□	·	·	·	·	·	Sid. time noon G.M.T.		12	57	29
												Interval *TO/FROM* noon p.m.			30	
												Result		12	57	29
	AC		·	·	·	·	·	·	·	·		Acceleration on interval p.m.				5
	MC	♂	·	✓	·	·						Sid. time at Greenwich at birth		12	57	34
												Longitude equivalent *+W*				
												LOCAL SID. TIME AT BIRTH		12	57	14
												Subtract 24 hrs. if necessary				

* Delete whichever is not required.

PETER MURRAY

his hot temper with maturity and I have to admit that I have never seen him lose his cool. Jupiter was rising in Capricorn when he was born, which gives him a grasp of big business and an affinity with large organizations, while the proximity of Saturn to the ascendant keeps his nose to the grindstone and makes him even more able than the average Virgoan to cope with details. I feel that he could be possessive and jealous in personal relationships due to his Venus in Scorpio, but this may be muted by its position in the 11th house. He may be ambivalent about marriage, wanting the closeness of Venus in a Water sign but also wanting the freedom and independence of the 11th house and the Sagittarian ascendant.

It is interesting to note that the sign which appears most frequently in the charts of broadcasters is Sagittarius, and that so many of them have either the Sun, Moon or ascendant in this sign. Even a midheaven in Sagittarius can lead to a career on the airwaves. It is also interesting to note that Pete and I work very comfortably together despite the fact that we have to cope with a live phone-in show on the fastest moving and most professional radio station in the country. No doubt we are helped by the fact that both our Mercuries are in conjunction in the 'think-on-your-feet' sign of Virgo.

♎ Libra

Ruled by Venus   **24 September — 23 October**

This sign is masculine, Cardinal and Airy in quality, suggesting a tough, outgoing, decisive personality with a muscular intellect. However, Librans are supposed to be gentle, loving, indecisive, longing for marriage and family life and more interested in hanging curtains than taking the world by storm. So, what went wrong?

This is a strange sign which encompasses some very gentle people who find it hard to assert themselves as well as some real tough nuts. Being an Air sign, Librans find it hard to cope with strong emotions and they become embarrassed and unnerved by tears or anger. They prefer to live and work in a peaceful atmosphere and will make quite an effort to fit in with others. However, Librans are also extremely independent and somehow manage to walk their own road through any circumstances and emerge centred, self-assured and apparently unchanged by all that has happened to them. Cardinality can express itself through the kind of determination to do things one's own way. This is demonstrated so admirably by one Libran, former Prime Minister Margaret Thatcher, but it can also emerge as an *appearance* of co-operation while going on to do just what one feels like. Libra natives are very bright, varying from intellectual to intuitive, shrewd to manipulative, street-wise to ivory-towered. Their brains work efficiently, but they are directed towards solving their *own* problems and making their own lives comfortable and meaningful rather than wasting mental energy on the needs of others. When faced with a weak and dependent personality or a person who wants to harp on about his own problems, the Libran's eyes glaze over with boredom. Well-centred and self-contained, these subjects march to their own drum-beat and underneath the soft exterior they are surprisingly tough. Even the apparently soft, gentle and disorganized Libran is really moulding his environment to suit himself.

The greatest and most obvious Libran attribute is charm. They make wonderful diplomats and public relations officers, never putting a foot wrong and never upsetting anyone. They are masters of the art of negotiating and can leave an adversary with his pride intact but with an uneasy feeling that he has agreed to everything that the Libran wanted. Socially, Librans are the greatest; they have a non-hostile approach to strangers and can disarm the hostility of others. They love to chat and also to listen carefully to the views of others, and they make the most wonderful house-guests. Librans are quite genuine in their admiration of those who have achieved something, and rarely feel jealous or put out by this. Librans don't seek the limelight, indeed they may appear unambitious, but they *do* like money. These natives need to live in tasteful surroundings with all the comforts and mod-cons laid on. Their homes are likely to be fully equipped with good music systems and the latest means of cooking. Everything about their homes, including the garden, is attractive and tidy. They need space and like to live near trees and fresh air. Librans make excellent lawyers. They can argue a point from all sides and do so in a manner which is both authoritative and pleasant. They hate to see an injustice and, although not the most energetic of signs, will fight to see justice done. These people are better at dealing with abstract political concepts than with dramas in their own family. They resist having pressure put on them and will either refuse point blank to be coerced or will slide out of harm's way. As for the famed Libran indecisiveness, I have discovered that some Librans cannot make a decision at all, while others simply like to take their time over this and, having decided, they can stick to their guns. Before becoming a full-time astrologer, I spent a few years working for a Libran who ran a very large employment agency. He taught me never to make an important decision on the spot or when upset or angry, but always to ask for 24 hours to think things over first. I have on many occasions since found this to be excellent advice.

As family members, Librans vary in their attitude. Most are very loving, caring and helpful and they don't stand in the way of an ambitious partner's career. Both sexes are very domesticated and capable of running a household beautifully, but they don't make the rest of the family suffer due to unreasonably high standards. Librans can make or mend anything and are probably capable of building a house for themselves and their families from scratch. They can be quite economical homemakers but they are neither miserly nor spendthrift, preferring a balance in this, as in all other things. Libran subjects are always ready to go out to a social event and they usually have at least one outside interest. Many are attached to organizations such as the girl guides or masonic clubs, while others enjoy light sports such as golf or tennis. These are reasonable people who are easy to live with, although they may be shallow and unable to understand the needs and emotions of others. They cannot live with anybody who makes demands upon them or dictates to them how they live. Neither will they stand for being questioned too closely about their whereabouts or their intentions. As parents, they are kind and reasonable. They are unlikely to cling to their children because they themselves are independent and will tend to foster a similar level of independence in their offspring. They encourage their children to appreciate art, culture, beauty and music because they themselves enjoy it so much.

The Duchess of York   15 October 1959

Sarah, Duchess of York, has her Sun, Mars and north node in Libra. The Sun/Mars conjunction in the 12th house makes her both strong and gentle at the same time. The conjunction gives her a hot temper and an impulsiveness which is more akin to Aries than Libra. However the 12th house stellium — Neptune and Mercury are also in the 12th — suggests that she has a mystical and creative nature and that she likes to be alone from time to time. Sarah is certainly creative and interested in the arts, having worked in publishing, been involved with fine arts and also written some children's books herself. It is interesting that her Moon is in the house which rules creativity and children's interests. Whatever path her life had taken, she would probably have chosen to work in these fields. The outgoing and adventurous image along with her red hair is typified by the hard aspect between the Sun and Mars while Jupiter rising in the 1st house in Sagittarius gives her a spirit of adventure and a need for personal freedom. The Moon in Aries (which can also bestow red hair) adds to the adventurousness and makes her a bit too masculine in outlook to be a stay-at-home housewife. A Scorpio ascendant assures us that whatever image she cares to project, something far deeper and more interesting is hiding behind it. Saturn in the 2nd house in Capricorn will bring considerable frustration as it seems that it could be many years before she will be able to fulfil her own destiny and make her own choices in life. The heavy emphasis on the 12th and the Scorpio ascendant suggests that it may be a long time before she is free to do her own thing, unfettered by her royal position.

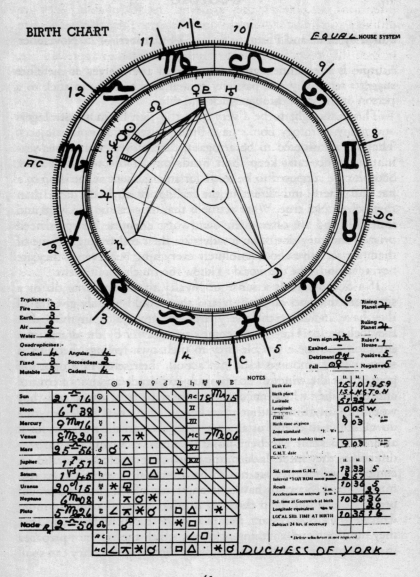

♏ Scorpio

Ruled by Mars and Pluto   **24 October — 22 November**

Scorpio is a feminine sign which is Fixed and Watery. It therefore suggests sensitivity and passivity as well as the ability to stick to a person or situation through thick and thin.

This is thought to be a very powerful sign by most astrologers and many astrology books have little praise for Scorpio subjects. They are considered to be arrogant, determined, obnoxious sex-maniacs who can't keep their heads out of the whisky bottle. Scorpios are supposed to be ready for an argument at the drop of a hat and utterly indifferent to the feelings of anybody other than themselves. Not true. What *is* true is that they can be awkward and inflexible and are often their own worst enemies. Scorpios need privacy and they don't like to advertise their real feelings. Some of them are secretive about absolutely everything but, even if they are not, they don't like the world to know too much about them.

If a Scorpio feels a sense of loyalty to a person, a job or a situation, this goes all the way and they would happily give up all they have, including their very lives, for anyone or anything that they believe in. They can become carried away by the drama of a situation and are a terrible prey to their own feelings, because as soon as their emotions kick into action, their sense of proportion goes out of the window. Scorpio subjects exude an aura of control and capability which encourages others to trust them and they would do anything rather than betray such trust or let anyone down. If put in charge of an enterprise, they do their utmost for it and try to steer the best possible course through whatever difficulties they meet. Indeed, they thrive on problems and also on competition but they are not so hard on their competitors as one might expect. Scorpios have a strong sense of fair play and would prefer to heal and help those in trouble rather than cause more damage than is necessary. Scorpios make excellent bosses in that they don't demand anything of others which they are not prepared to do themselves, and no one works harder. However, they can spoil this good impression be being insensitive; for example, by making a subordinate feel stupid or by refusing to acknowledge the difficulties under which he is working. They are capable of sacrificing others in order to achieve a particular end but, to be fair, they will try to minimize this sacrifice as much as possible. As subordinates, they are loyal and hardworking and rarely stab others in the back. They can use their considerable intelligence to manipulate people and situations around to their way of thinking and they can tune out the things that they don't like. Scorpios can display a very charming and attractive manner when they need to. They have an arresting appearance and may even be beautiful to look at, with thick wavy hair and lovely well-modulated voices.

Scorpios have considerable courage and endurance. They can face up to almost insurmountable difficulties without giving in and they can hold on tenaciously to what they consider to be theirs. They stick to jobs, homes, relationships and their money for as long as possible and they don't easily forgive anyone who parts them from anything which they value. They don't see the need for change and will usually try to mend something rather than throw it out and get something new. Scorpios make excellent doctors, nurses and psychiatrists but they ignore their own illnesses. They have no love for weak and dependent people and, although they are good listeners, are contemptuous of those who choose to wallow in self-pity. And yet, for all their appearance of strength and hatred of weakness, they are not as strong as they look. Scorpios can become extremely depressed and may even turn to alcohol during their worst moments. They are also first-class sulks who, when they get themselves into an angry mood, don't know how to get themselves out of it. Their pride and hatred of being seen as weak make it hard for them to apologize or to admit that they have behaved less than admirably. Yet they need to be loved. Scorpios seem to miss out on their share of love during childhood, often by having a hard or uncaring mother and a weak ineffective father. They find it difficult to make relationships and may substitute sex for feeling. When they do get around to marriage and family life, they try their hardest to make this a success. Many Scorpios have terrible marriages but even more of them have excellent relationships. There doesn't seem to be a middle ground. I am not sure about their sexy reputation. Some Scorpios use sex as a form of emotional release but others like to be thought of as sexy while in fact they are rather prudish. They can say quite outrageous things in order to shock others.

Scorpios can be very loving parents and they try to do all that they can for their children. They can be over-demanding, however, and may lack the softness which a small child requires. If the Scorpio becomes the parent of a headstrong and sporty Aries child, this can result in a magnificent relationship in which the adult does all he or she can to foster the child's talents. However, if the child is a gentle and fussy Virgo, the parent may never learn to respect or understand him and may bully him unmercifully. Scorpios can be the best or the worst of people and they take a lot of understanding. If you live with one, you must stand up to him or he will never respect or understand you.

John Cleese   **27 October 1939**

With the Sun, Mars and Mercury in Scorpio, actor, comedian and writer John Cleese is probably fairly typical of his sign. I say probably because, apart from his public persona, do we know what he is really like? His ability to parody the stupidity of others and to make a point by comic means hides his real persona perfectly. He would probably squirm if put into a psychiatrist's chair, but despite this his Moon in Aries denotes that he would open out to those whom he trusts. The Aries/Scorpio mixture could have led him to a career as a great military leader but this would depend upon the position of Mars in juxtaposition with either the ascendant or the midheaven. His Mars, incidentally, is in the charming and business-minded sign of Libra, so he is well able to use his intelligence and energy for business purposes. It is interesting to note that he began a successful alternative career in producing training packs for business during the 1960s, at a time when making money was considered to be infra dig. The fact that his friends accused him of being a crypto-facist didn't influence him one bit. Having made up his mind to this course of action, he stuck to his guns — very Scorpio.

BIRTH CHART

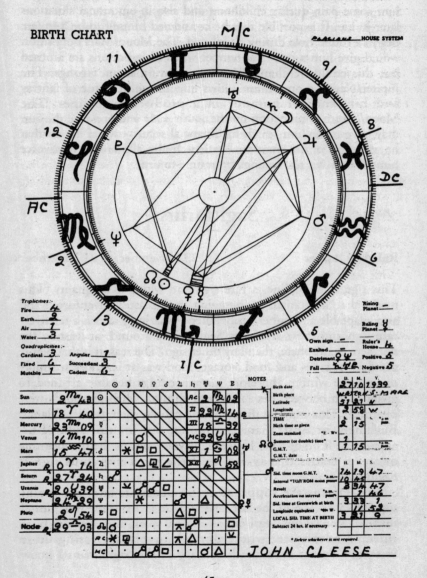

The conjunction of John's Moon with Saturn must have brought him some pain during childhood and also in emotional situations later in life. It is possible that he considered himself to be a square peg in a round hole during childhood. The Moon/Mars opposition would give him a powerful temper when his emotions are aroused but this could be channelled into righting social wrongs. The Jupiter/Neptune opposition allows him to use his sense of fantasy and his sense of humour in a productive manner. The Moon/Saturn conjunction on the south node and opposite the Sun may have made him search for financial security when he felt that he was short of the emotional variety. It also allows him to divorce himself from his real feelings from time to time.

♐ Sagittarius

Ruled by Jupiter   **23 November — 21 December**

This sign is masculine, a Fire sign and Mutable in quality. This means that Sagittarians are outgoing, enthusiastic, adventurous and also adaptable and rather easily bored. Amazingly, this is a relatively rare sign and there are fewer Sagittarians around, at least in the northern hemisphere, than any other sign. The reason is that before the days of cities and food storage, food was at its shortest supply during the winter, therefore human beings became attuned to giving birth between the spring and autumn when foodstuffs were plentiful. This may be different for people such as the Kalahari Bushmen, or Australian Aborigines, but for the bulk of us, apparently, it holds true. However, if you work in the broadcasting or travel trades it may feel as if the most populous sign is Sagittarius.

Sagittarians are supposed to be outdoor, freedom-loving explorers who live in the fast lane and are at the same time deeply involved in religious, legal or educational work. But, the idea of an intrepid adventurer whose day job involves dressing up in vestments doesn't seem much like any of the Sagittarians I know!

Outwardly, Sagittarians are the most pleasant of people because they have an open approach and genuinely enjoy making new friends. They are also extremely generous, even when they are broke. Sagittarians can be tactless: they don't mean to hurt, it is just that they are extremely honest and such honesty can be a little hard to take. Most Fire sign people are enthusiastic and adventurous but the Sagittarian is particularly noted for this. He is also optimistic, cheerful and rarely depressed. Oddly enough these subjects lack confidence in themselves and frequently attach themselves to what they consider to be stronger personalities. They are good company, fit in pretty easily with others and can adapt to almost any kind of circumstance. However, they are quite fussy and won't live or work in difficult circumstances for longer than absolutely necessary. They enjoy meeting a constant stream of new people or dealing with clients on the telephone. Therefore Sagittarians seek out jobs where they can do this and where, if possible, they can help people. They can be quite nasty if attacked, but their anger quickly dissolves because they tend to put all experience behind them and move right on to the next thing.

Traditionally, Sagittarians are supposed to like the outdoors and to be especially keen on horses. While this is certainly true for some, the sense of freedom to get out into the country whenever they want is enough for others. They like to retire to sunny places where they can live in the open air and play sports all year round. Most of these subjects love to travel and many of them work in the travel trade because, although it pays badly, it offers opportunities for cheap travel. Many Sagittarians leave the country of their birth and live elsewhere, frequently marrying into a different culture than that of their birth. They are totally at ease with people of every race and colour and find the differences between people fascinating and never a cause for suspicion or fear.

Many Sagittarians are quite athletic, enjoying sports, dancing, acrobatics or horse-riding throughout their lives. How successful they are as competitors depends upon other factors on their charts, because the Sun sign alone may lack the determination which is needed to be a winner. These people do like to shine, however, and many of them seek a career in the entertainment business where their looks, talent and sense of humour stand them in good stead. They continue to educate themselves throughout life and also to pick up new ideas and methods as they go along. As workmates they are fun, but they may lack (or appear to lack) the dedication which a particular job demands, and they are not keen on the messier part of any job. In both working and personal situations, they may take on more than they can cope with and then become worn out and ill as a result. These subjects want to help humanity and may therefore take jobs as teachers, counsellors and astrologers, for example. Others have a strong spiritual tendency which may take them into the Church or to mediumistic and healing work.

Some Sagittarians are too keen on personal freedom to be able to cope with a deep personal relationship except on a short-term basis. Others seem to take on the responsibility for the whole family and then find that they cannot cope with it. If they are allowed to play the field for a good few years before settling down, they make excellent partners. They may be a bit daft at times but they are never boring. Their friends tend to come and go but they are loyal to their families. Sagittarians make imaginative parents who want their children to be both free and happy and the only time problems arise is if the children are particularly clingy, nervous or needy. As friends and as partners, they are best if they are left to do their own thing and neither smothered with love nor asked to account for their movements. In many ways, Sagittarian lives are different, because they tend to have values which are spiritual rather than material and to want to enjoy life rather than to acquire material goods.

Ian Botham   **24 November 1955**

Ian is a typical Sagittarian; tall, sporty and humorous but also hot tempered and too honest for some people's taste. In fact, his Sun is only just into Sagittarius although Venus in the same sign adds to his love of freedom and his pleasant manner. To reach the top in any sport requires a good deal of dedication and very hard work in addition to talent. His Sagittarian planets give him the talent and the dash that he needs, but it is the presence of Saturn and Mercury

BIRTH CHART

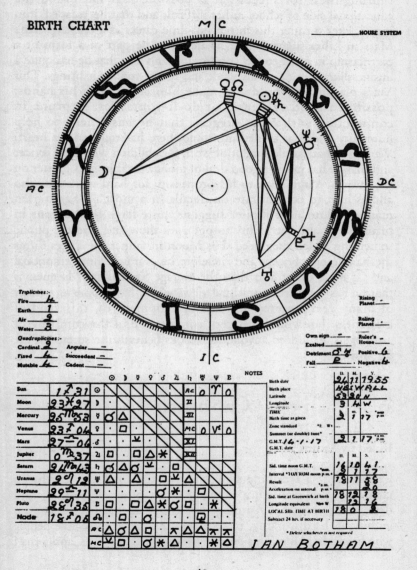

49

in conjunction in Scorpio which give the necessary tenacity and thoroughness for success. It is possible that Ian found the educational side of school rather difficult and that he 'escaped' into sports, later turning this into a full-time career as a cricketer. Ian's Mars in Libra suggests that he needs to be part of a team or a partnership in order to feel comfortable and also that he has quite a businesslike attitude to his work and to the money it brings. This Mars placement would also make him clever with his hands, possibly a good carpenter or do-it-yourselfer. Neptune in conjunction with Mars suggests that he has a need to help humanity and that something somewhere has touched his heart. We know that Ian does a lot of work for children who have cancer and that he has raised a good deal of money for this. Ian's Jupiter on the cusp of Virgo adds to his propensity for hard work and also allows him to concentrate on details in a most un-Sagittarian manner. Pluto near Jupiter suggests quite large fluctuations in finances but also the ability to put on a show and give the public something which they need. His Moon in vulnerable Pisces forms the handle of a bucket and therefore he is much more emotional and far more easily hurt than the average Sagittarian. My guess is that he has very strong spiritual views which have come as a result of many years interest in, and development of, this kind of awareness. Ian would feel very comfortable in the company of astrologers, or indeed anyone who looks beneath the surface of life for answers.

♑   # Capricorn

Ruled by Saturn   **22 December — 20 January**

Capricorn is a feminine sign which is Cardinal and Earthy in character. This makes it a strange mixture of gentle passivity and determined assertion. Astrology books tell us that Capricorns are ambitious, hard-working, materialistic and rather miserable people who have a hard life. This doesn't sound much like the Capricorns I know, but perhaps I'm prejudiced. I rather like Capricorns; I feel comfortable with them and I trust them. Capricorns are shy and retiring, they don't push themselves forward and they feel embarrassed if they are put on show in any way. They make very good backroom boys, working away on a project without making a fuss about anything. This doesn't mean that they can be pushed around, for they are very obstinate and perfectly capable of saying no when they feel it necessary. These people can be very tough in business but they are rarely unreasonable. Capricorns are patient, realistic and responsible. Like all Earth sign people, they like to work at their own pace and hate to be rushed and hassled. Many Capricorns are ambitious and status conscious; they want to get on and they want to see their families succeed as well. Capricorns have no time for loafers or scroungers.

The biggest hurdle which these subjects have to overcome is their childhood. They are often painfully shy and may be teased by more outgoing children. They are clever and usually do well at school but they lack confidence and need to be encouraged or they can fall by the wayside. If a Capricorn does have a bad start, either due to school, family circumstances or ill health, he usually catches up later on. Capricorns are attracted to business and also to the details of any work which they do. Many are scientifically minded. while others love maths. Their memories are excellent and they are rarely ruffled by problems at work. One point which is never mentioned in astrology books is their excellent public relations skills. Capricorns excel at dealing with people and make wonderful liaison managers. They have considerable charm and a wonderful dry sense of humour which is never hurtful, and they are sensitive to the feelings of others. The world of publishing fascinates Capricorns because it has that magic mixture of business, details and interesting people.

Capricorns may take their jobs and their family responsibilities seriously but that does not mean that they are boring. They know how to enjoy themselves, particularly later in life. These subjects love to travel and explore, as long as they are fairly comfortable while doing so. They enjoy gentle sports, dancing, amateur dramatics and many other surprisingly active hobbies. Their sense of responsibility makes them careful with money but they can go overboard with a business enterprise or become so involved with details that they lose sight of the overall pattern and lose money as a result. These subjects can also lose money by supporting those members of their families who lean on them. Sometimes they can be too long-suffering for their own good.

Capricorns make excellent marriage partners just as long as they are appreciated. They are steadfast and loyal and maybe a little dull but they really care for their families. These subjects are very good with older people and never leave elderly parents or even their in-laws in the lurch. They will even take care of someone whom they really don't like, rather than abandoning them. Their lack of confidence often leads them to team up with stronger personalities who they feel would look after them. If they find a supportive and caring partner, then the relationship turns out fine, but if they find themselves attached to a bully or to someone who hides weakness with an appearance of strength, then they will be very unhappy and it takes a lot to make them leave a marriage. Also, despite their diffidence and feelings of insecurity, it is well to remember that this is a Cardinal sign, and therefore not likely to be pushed about all that much. Capricorns are quite flirtatious and like to attract the opposite sex, but this is rarely meant as anything more than a bit of party-time fun. It is easy for Capricorns to flirt, as they are often good looking and very pleasant to be with. As parents, these people are serious, gentle and encouraging. They want their children to get on and they will sacrifice a good deal for this. They may not be much good at playing rough sports with their children but they will sit and read to them or help them with their homework as best they can. These subjects tend to live a long time and are often happier and more successful in old age than when young. Many continue to be friends and companions to their children over the years.

Capricorns can be mean and far too materialistic and can see others as potential providers of money. They may only be mean to themselves but quite generous to their loved ones but some become so money-minded that they lose their sense of proportion. They can also become so wrapped up in what they are trying to achieve that they begin to believe that the end justifies the means. Some

Capricorns can be terrible moaners who whine about everything and worry endlessly about everything and nothing. I once had a Capricorn client who wanted me to tell her which date would be the most propitious for her to visit the hairdressers and have blond streaks put in. This is a good example of someone who takes little things far too far and loses any kind of feeling for others or any sense of proportion. Fortunately, most Capricorns are not so self absorbed or silly.

Rowan Atkinson   6 January 1955

The elegant comedian Rowan Atkinson may not have chosen a typically Capricornian career but I understand that he does as much, if not more, behind the scenes as he does in front of them. He has reached the top of his career because he is a hard worker with a strong sense of responsibility. Rowan's Venus and Saturn in Scorpio add to his dedication and tenacity but they also suggest a passionate and possessive side of his nature which we, the public, don't see. The tight conjunction of his Jupiter and Uranus in Cancer suggest that he could find some extremely original ways of earning a living, and this conjunction also accounts for his extraordinary talent and his off-beat way of looking at life. The same conjunction may also suggest that he can go off at a tangent, suddenly changing his mind, becoming unreliable and behaving in a very un-Capricornian manner.

His Mars in Pisces makes him gentle and creative but also a fighter for what he considers right. He would hate to be taken advantage of by anyone. Rowan's Moon in Gemini could have added to the usual Capricorn loneliness during childhood because he could have felt like a square peg in a round hole and, even if his family were loving and kind to him, he may have suffered from bullying or feeling of apartness at school. The Moon in Gemini suggests that he can be a little cool or reluctant to become closely involved with others, possibly because he knows he can go over the top in relationships due to those planets in the emotional sign of Scorpio. Rowan's trine between Venus and Mars gives him enough charm to get away with almost anything, but he would have to work hard at any close relationships.

BIRTH CHART

HOUSE SYSTEM _____

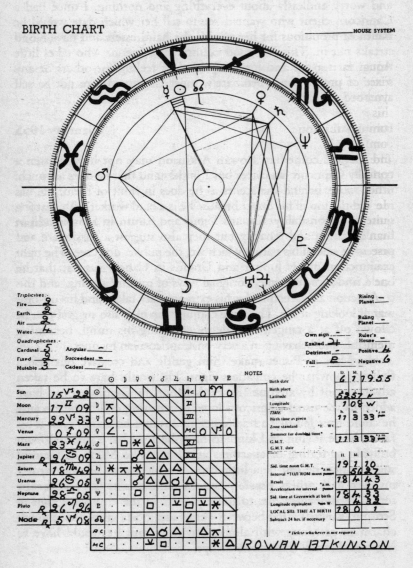

Triplicities
Fire — 2
Earth — 2
Air — 2
Water — 4

Quadruplicities
Cardinal — 5
Fixed — 2
Mutable — 3

Angular —
Succeedent —
Cadent —

Rising —
Planet

Ruling —
Planet

Own sign —
Exalted — 24
Detriment —
Fall — P

Ruler's —
House

Positive — 6
Negative — 6

NOTES

	☉	☽	☿	♀	♂	♃	♄	♅	♆	♇										
Sun	15 ♑ 22	☉										AC	0	♋	0					
Moon	17 ♊ 09	☽	↗									II								
Mercury	22 ♑ 33	☿										III								
Venus	0 ♒ 09	♀	□									MC	0	♑	0					
Mars	23 ♓ 44	♂	·	□	✳							XI								
Jupiter	℞ 26 ♌ 09	♃	·	✳	·	⚹	△	△				XII								
Saturn	18 ♏ 49	♄	✳	↗	✳	·	△	△												
Uranus	26 ♋ 05	♅	·	⚹	·	□	△	△	△											
Neptune	26 ♎ 05	♆	·	□	·	□	△	·	□	□										
Pluto	℞ 26 ♌ 26	♇	·	□	·	□	↯	↯	△	✳										
Node	℞ 5 ♑ 08	☊							↗											
		AC			△	☌	△		△	↗										
		MC	·	↯	□	·	✳	△			✳	△								

Birth date	6	1	1955
Birth place			
Latitude	52	57	N
Longitude	1	08	W

	h.	m.	s.
TIME			
Birth time as given	11	3	33 a.m.
Zone standard *E W			
Summer (or double) time*			
G.M.T.	11	3	33 a.m.
G.M.T. date			

	H.	M.	S.
Sid. time noon G.M.T.	19	1	10 a.m./p.m.
Interval *TO/FROM noon a.m./p.m.		56	27
Result	78	43	
Acceleration on interval a.m./p.m.			10
Sid. time at Greenwich at birth	78	43	33
Longitude equivalent E W		43	32
LOCAL SID. TIME AT BIRTH	78	0	1
Subtract 24 hrs. if necessary			

* Delete whichever is not required

ROWAN ATKINSON

Aquarius

≈

Ruled by Uranus and Saturn   **21 January — 19 February**

Aquarius is a masculine sign which has the element of Air and is Fixed in nature. Some people get a little confused because the star symbol for Aquarius is a man pouring water from a pot, but despite this it is an Air sign and not a Water one. This masculine, Fixed Air combination makes for a stubborn and decisive character who feels comfortable in the realm of ideas but who may find the nurturing and feeling side of his nature difficult to deal with. A friend once commented to me that, although both he, his wife and a number of other members of his family were Aquarians, they were all different. He then asked how astrology accounted for this? The answer is quite simple. In the first place, there is much more on any chart than the Sun sign to account for someone's nature and that, in the case of Aquarians, being *different* is the nature of the sign. For example, a group of Aquarians would be far more different from one another than a group of Taureans would be.

Aquarians are independent and sometimes quite eccentric. They march to their own drumbeat and live to their own rules. They also allow others around them to enjoy *their* own space and to be themselves, although most Aquarians are convinced that their own ideas are the right ones. These people are often very successful in their chosen fields, partly because they have the ability to concentrate on what they choose to do despite any distractions which may be around them. They are extremely creative, especially in the realm of ideas and are the very best people to discuss things with, although some of them lack the practicality to carry their own tasks through to a conclusion. Aquarians are clever, friendly, kind and humane and they make the best possible friends. They may not turn out to be really reliable when the chips are down because they are too strongly tuned to their own needs to want to live someone else's life for them. They can be like the politician who spouts ideals on behalf of humanity but lives by quite different rules when it comes to himself. Aquarians make wonderful teachers because they pass on their fascination with their subject to others and they love to foster talent. However, these subjects don't like competition and when someone seems to overtake them at their own game they become extremely put out.

Aquarians have an unsentimental and detached attitude which can seem impersonal and even tactless at times; however, their clarity of thinking is more valuable to their many friends than cloying sentimentality. These subjects are inventors and innovators whose interest in any technical subject is easily aroused. They are good at a great many things and can make practically anything with their hands when they are in the right mood. Their opinions can be fixed, although they will always respond to reasoned argument and they are tolerant of the opinions of others. Aquarians could never be racist or chauvinistic because they are too fascinated by the world and everyone in it. Many Aquarians are animal lovers who take on the care of sick or dependent animals with great dedication. These subjects are unafraid of authority figures and are rarely influenced by other more powerful people. They don't follow and they may not lead; they prefer to take their own road at all times. Many Aquarians are self-employed, working as artists, writers and inventors. Others will find a job they like and stick to it for years without appearing unduly ambitious, and then will suddenly change tack completely, going into a totally different line of work. It is impossible to suggest a typically Aquarian job — I have Aquarian friends who are farmers, trainers and breeders of horses, professional astrologers, publishers, business-people and ministers of the Church. The link is that they are all passionately interested in what they are doing and really care about the results of their work.

Aquarians are usually very successful in close personal relationships. They need to choose a partner who is capable, tolerant and who has a full life of his or her own. They cannot live with a weak or overly emotional type, although they are often drawn to people who will do their emoting for them, so to speak. These subjects may have to experiment with a relationship or two before finding just the right person to live with, but once they have done so they stick to their partner through thick and thin. It is almost unheard of for an Aquarian to be unfaithful and it goes completely against the grain for them to tell lies or to live in a dishonest relationship. If they find themselves becoming more interested in someone other than their partner, they would be completely open about it, even if it meant losing both relationships. These subjects can change their lifestyles completely if they are seriously unhappy. Aquarians cannot take too much routine in family life, as they need to be able to take off at a moment's notice and not to be tied down to a list of chores.

As a parent, the Aquarian will give his children every possible opportunity to develop their talents and their minds. It doesn't matter what subject a child chooses to become interested in, the Aquarian parent will be behind him all the way. The Aquarian may find it hard to cope with an unhappy child because he backs away from emotional problems and doesn't understand how to deal with them. Quite a number of Aquarians choose not to have children at all because they know they would find it hard to cope with them. Others have them and somehow seem to drift away from them. leaving the other parent or someone else to bring them up.

Marti Caine   **26 January 1945**

Marti's Sun is on its own in Aquarius suggesting that other factors on her chart would play a strong a part in her character. Her Mercury and Mars are in conjunction in hard-working Capricorn which gives her the self-discipline which she needs as a professional entertainer to finish all that she starts. This conjunction also helps her to bring her wonderful ideas to fruition. The combination of Sun in Aquarius and Moon in Cancer would make her a good teacher and I wonder if she has ever considered making her living in this way. She would also be a tireless worker for a cause because the Cancer/Capricorn emphasis would make her keen to preserve everything that is worth while. Venus in Pisces brings a gentle artistry and creativity to all her work while the closeness of Saturn to the Moon brings a necessary attention to detail. Marti's tall, slim good looks and elegance are typically Aquarian while her strong, camera-friendly looks reflect her Capricornian planets. Jupiter and

BIRTH CHART

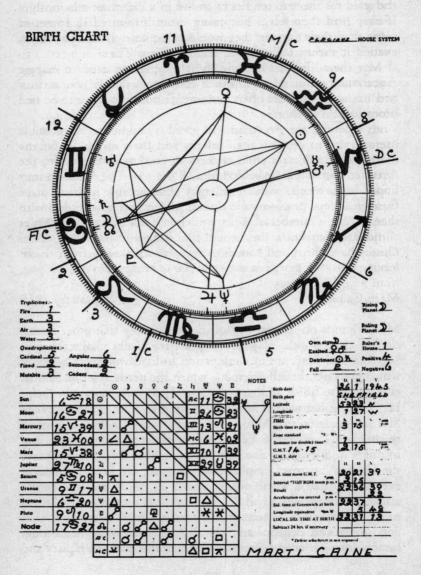

PLACIDUS HOUSE SYSTEM

Triplicities:-
Fire — 1
Earth — 3
Air — 3
Water — 3

Quadruplicities:-
Cardinal — 5   Angular — 6
Fixed — 2   Succeedent — 2
Mutable — 3   Cadent — 2

Rising Planet ☽
Ruling Planet ☽

Own sign ☽   Ruler's House 1
Exalted ♃♈   Positive 4
Detriment ⊙♑   Negative 6
Fall ♇

	⊙	☽	☿	♀	♂	♃	♄	♅	♆	♇					NOTES
Sun	6 ♒ 18	⊙									AC	11 ♋ 39		
Moon	16 ♋ 27	☽		☌							II	26 ♋ 23		
Mercury	15 ♑ 39	☿			☌	△					III	13 ♌ 21		
Venus	23 ♓ 00	♀	∠	△							MC	6 ♓ 02		
Mars	15 ♑ 38	♂		☌	☌						XI	10 ♈ 39		
Jupiter	27 ♏ 10	♃									XII	29 ♉ 39		
Saturn	5 ♊ 08	♄	⊼				□							
Uranus	9 ♊ 17	♅	△				☌							
Neptune	6 ♎ 20	♆					□	△						
Pluto	9 ♌ 10	♇				⊡			⁎					
Node	17 ♒ 27	☊	·	☌	☌	△	·							
	AC		☌	·	☌	△	·	□	·					
	MC	♅				·	△	⊡	·					

Birth date — 26 . 1 . 1945
Birth place — SHEFFIELD
Latitude — 53 23 N
Longitude — 1 27 W
TIME
Birth time as given —
Zone standard *E. W —
Summer (or double) time* —
G.M.T. 14·15
G.M.T. date —

	H.	M.	
Birth time as given	3	15	p.m.
Summer (or double) time*	2	16	p.m.

	H.	M.	S.
Sid. time noon G.M.T.	20	21	39
Interval *TO/FROM noon p.m.	2	15	
Result	22	36	39
Acceleration on interval p.m.			22
Sid. time at Greenwich at birth	22	37	1
Longitude equivalent *E. W		5	48
LOCAL SID. TIME AT BIRTH	22	31	13
Subtract 24 hrs. if necessary			

* Delete whichever is not required

MARTI CAINE

Neptune in conjunction on the Virgo/Libra cusp add to her looks and grace, while the trine between Neptune and Uranus bring a spark of genius to her comic talent. Marti's Moon and Saturn in Cancer show that she needs a settled home with a steady relationship and an old-fashioned kind of family life.

Marti was very ill during 1989, fighting the dreaded disease cancer. The transit of Saturn over her Mercury/Mars conjunction and opposite her natal Moon coincide with this struggle. The Moon, especially in the sign of Cancer can be very sensitive to the kinds of hormonal changes which cause cells to attack the body. Mercury is very much associated with health and is often at the heart of any serious illness, especially when Neptune is added to the mixture. In this case, the presence of Neptune and also Uranus opposite her natal Saturn added to the problems. The worst of these transits is now over but she may have a few more problems to face as Neptune and Uranus pass over the Mercury/Mars conjunction during 1991 and 1992. On the other hand, these transits could bring unexpected benefits her way rather than more health problems. Let's hope that this is so, and that her career goes from strength to strength.

♓ Pisces

Ruled by Neptune and Jupiter   **20 February — 20 March**

Pisces is a feminine sign which is Mutable in character and of the Water element. This is the softest, most pliable and feminine of all the signs and therefore vulnerable, able to nurture people and animals and supposedly lacking in aggression. Pisceans are supposed to be dreamy incompetents who are drunk a good deal of the time. If this doesn't sound like any of the Pisceans who you know, I'm not really surprised. This sign has an undeservedly bad press.

These kindly people work very hard at their chosen careers as long as the job allows them to do something for others. Many

Pisceans are excellent teachers while others work in the field of health or counselling, but they do need variety in their work. Pisceans are astute business people whose intuition helps them make gains and avoid pitfalls. Despite their unworldly image, they like money and some of them manage to make quite a lot of it. These subjects can also be surprisingly mean in small ways while being generous to those whom they love. Problems come when they lose interest in what they are doing or if things start to go wrong, because they lack the kind of determination which would keep them going through times of trouble. Piscean confidence can suddenly evaporate, leaving them unable to cope or even to protect themselves from danger. These subjects need a practical, supportive, encouraging partner at work and also in their private life if they are going to be successful.

The great Piscean virtue is their intuition and their natural understanding of people and their needs. These subjects can be so receptive to other people's feelings that they become tangled up in them and don't know which emotion belongs to them and which has been taken on board on behalf of someone else. Pisceans are rarely tactless but they can be quite hurtful if they feel threatened. These subjects are clever, resourceful, often artistic, always creative and more capable than they are given credit for. However, their achilles heel is a lack of confidence and a tendency to be overwhelmed by stronger, more pushy personalities. Pisceans can suffer from the attentions of bullies or those who seek to use and manipulate them, but they also have the ability to slide out of a situation if it doesn't suit them.

A Piscean's home is his castle. It may be a palace or a tiny apartment but he feels strongly about it and he will usually try to live in pleasant surroundings. Oddly enough, Pisceans often spend quite long spells of their life in an atmosphere which may look attractive but which lacks emotional harmony. These subjects like to be surrounded by friends, family members and animals and are always glad to have visitors or to get out and visit others. They also need time to themselves in order to replenish their nervous energy. Pisceans love conversation and make excellent friends, but their nerves are quite delicate so they try to avoid those who have too many problems and are apt to slip away if too many demands are made upon them. Most Pisceans are fond of food and drink and many are excellent cooks. They have a reputation for drinking too much and many of them do seem to go through phases of hitting the bottle, although most of them keep their drinking within reasonable limits, while some hardly drink at all. This is a hard sign to categorize. The tendency to drink comes from their need to escape from the harsh realities of life, but many of them find other avenues of escape, such as artistic or dramatic outlets. Many Pisceans are surprisingly strongly sexed for this too offers a chance to escape into ecstasy from time to time.

Most Pisceans are interested in those matters which are outside the normal realms of daily life. Therefore they become involved in New Age subjects such as astrology, Tarot, hypnotherapy, alternative medicine and alternative philosophies of many kinds. There is a strong need to understand those forces which cannot be experienced through the senses but of which they are aware. Pisceans make excellent mediums and spiritual healers, they seem to represent some kind of thread which joins the world of the spirit with the world of practical matters. I noticed on more than one occasion when working at one New Age event that every person around me had either the Sun, Moon or ascendant in Pisces.

Many Pisceans struggle with health problems or allergies. This is not a strong sign and these people seem to be given these times of illness in order to take them out of the rat race and allow them time to retreat and reflect. Their moods also take some getting used to because they can become very depressed on occasion without always being able to explain why. This depression may be due to some kind of change in the atmosphere around them or because they are soaking up someone else's unhappiness. Pisceans can be very self-sacrificing and can waste inordinate amounts of time and money on those whose needs appear to be greater than their own. Once again, this arises through their need to put the world and all the people in it to rights.

Pisceans have mixed fortunes in relationships. They are hard to understand and they also have a tendency to choose difficult partners, sometimes hopeless people, whom they try to rescue. If and when they can find the right partner, they grow in stature and achieve a great deal, but many of them seem to lack common sense when their feelings are aroused. These subjects love children and make wonderful parents, especially if their children are as sensitive and creative as they are. They cannot cope with determinedly difficult children and may give up on them, leaving stronger members of their families to bring them up. Many Pisceans find animals easier to deal with than children. Despite all this softness, Pisceans have a strong sense of self and a surprising amount of inner strength. Being a Mutable sign, they can walk away from a situation which is no longer viable and adapt to another one surprisingly quickly and far more successfully than other, stronger planetary types.

Paddy Ashdown   **27 February 1947**

Paddy Ashdown has the Sun, Mercury and the Moon in Pisces which should make him very soft and vulnerable. However, he is a top politician — leader of Britain's third largest political party — and an ex-commando. His three Piscean planets are in the 8th house which is a tough house, often associated with military matters through its connection with the planet Mars. Like so many politicians, Paddy's ascendant is in the proud and Fiery sign of Leo. This makes him idealistic and also keen on being the leader of any group he joins. Paddy has a stellium of Uranus, Saturn and Jupiter in Taurus in the 10th house at the top of his chart. Saturn in this position denotes public success, but also the possibility of public failure if his luck runs out. Jupiter in conjunction with Saturn suggests that his luck will not run out and the conjunction of these two planets creates a balance between the over-optimism and expansiveness of Jupiter with the depressive, limiting action of Saturn. Uranus in the 10th shows rather sudden changes of direction and sometimes a tendency towards revolutionary ways of reaching his aims. Paddy's opposition between the Moon and Neptune in the eighth and second houses brings ups and downs in connection with money. This situation would have made life difficult if Paddy had decided to go into business rather than

BIRTH CHART

7°P O C H Z... HOUSE SYSTEM

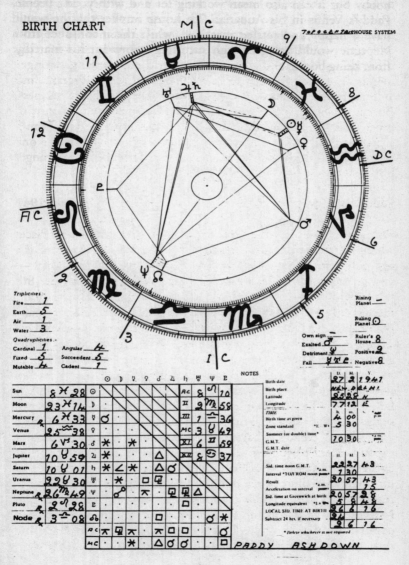

Triplicities:-
Fire _1_
Earth _5_
Air _1_
Water _3_

Quadruplicities:-
Cardinal _1_   Angular _4_
Fixed _5_   Succeedent _5_
Mutable _4_   Cadent _1_

Rising Planet —
Ruling Planet ☉

Own sign —   Ruler's House _8_
Exalted ♂   Positive _2_
Detriment ☿   Negative _8_
Fall ♃ ♅ ♀

NOTES

	☉	☽	☿	♀	♂	♃	♄	♅	♆	♇				
Sun	8 ♓ 28	☉									AC	8 ♌	10
Moon	23 ♓ 14	☽									II	9 ♍	58
Mercury ℞	6 ♓ 33	☿									III	7 ♎	36
Venus	25 ♒ 38	♀									MC	3 ♉	49
Mars	6 ♑ 30	♂									XI	6 ♊	59
Jupiter	10 ♉ 59	♃									XII	5 ♋	37
Saturn	10 ♉ 01	♄												
Uranus	22 ♉ 30	♅												
Neptune ℞	26 ♏ 49	♆												
Pluto ℞	2 ♌ 28	♇												
Node ℞	3 ♎ 08	☊												

	D	M	Y
Birth date	27	2	1947
Birth place	NEW DELHI		
Latitude	28 26		N
Longitude	77 12		E

TIME:		h.	m.	
Birth time as given		4	00	p.m.
Zone standard *E. W*		5	30	
Summer (or double) time*				a.m.
G.M.T.		10	30	a.m.
G.M.T. date				

	H	M	S
Sid. time noon G.M.T.	22	27	43
Interval *TO/FROM noon points*	7	30	
Result *a.m.	20	57	43
Acceleration on interval			15
Sid. time at Greenwich at birth	20	57	28
Longitude equivalent *E.*	5	8	48
LOCAL SID. TIME AT BIRTH	26	6	76
Subtract 24 hrs. if necessary	24		
	2	6	76

* Delete whichever is not required

PADDY ASHDOWN

63

politics. Mars in Capricorn in the 5th house could suggest a serious hobby but it can also mean working for and with young people. Paddy's Venus in his Aquarian 7th house implies that he would have a happy and settled marriage, while the inconjunct from Neptune would bring enough surprises to prevent his marriage from being boring.

CHAPTER TWO

CHART SHAPING, HEMISPHERES AND PLANETARY FEATURES

If you take a look at Billy Connolly's chart on page 74 and apply the ideas which are described here, you will have a fair idea of his character by the time you reach the end. In case you have never heard of him, Billy is a very funny and irreverent comedian from Glasgow in Scotland. Scottish charts are nice and accurate to work with because the Scots put the time of birth on their birth certificates.

When is a planet not a planet?

For the sake of simplicity, astrologers refer to the Sun and Moon as planets even though the Sun is a minor star and the Moon is a satellite of the Earth.

Chart shaping

The bowl

The shape of a chart can show how its energies are concentrated. The bowl shape means that all the planets are placed in one area of the chart, thereby emphasizing the signs, houses and the

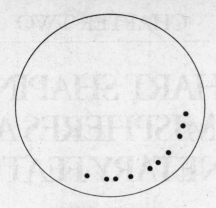

The bowl-shaped chart

hemispheres which they occupy. Occasionally one comes across a chart where almost all the planets are squeezed into one or two signs of the zodiac. People with this type of chart are one-sided, blinkered characters who tend to have one abiding interest at the expense of all others.

The bucket

A bucket chart has most of the planets in one area, with one or two planets placed on the opposite side. Such charts place an inordinately heavy emphasis on the one or two planets which are located on the 'handle' side of the bucket. This gives these planets a stronger influence on the chart than they otherwise would command.

The locomotive

A locomotive chart has planets placed in many signs; however, these are positioned at about the same degree of each of the signs. This means that the subject has a well-balanced and well-rounded personality. However, when a transiting planet comes across *one* of the natal planets, it makes aspects to all the others too. This means

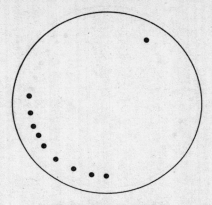

The bucket-shaped chart

that long periods of calm are interspersed by hectically eventful periods and battalions of problems.

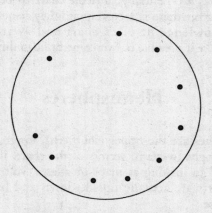

The locomotive-shaped chart

The see-saw

Another difficult chart is the see-saw, which has a bunch of planets (a stellium) in two opposing signs. This chart shows considerable

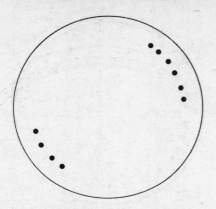

The see-saw-shaped chart

tension in the subject's personality which tends to surface whenever a major progression or transit is in action. There is no need for a subject who has a potentially difficult chart to be depressed; for every 'hard' transit there is a correspondingly beneficial one. Also, increased knowledge of one's chart and awareness of one's personality make it possible to overcome built-in difficulties.

Hemispheres

The hemispheres are the upper (southern), lower (northern), left (eastern) and right (western) sectors of the chart. If you are sharp-eyed and used to looking at maps or atlases, you will notice that astrology charts are actually upside-down and back-to-front in relation to these.

The upper (southern) hemisphere

The upper hemisphere contains the 7th, 8th, 9th, 10th, 11th and 12th houses. A subject who has most of his planets in this part of his chart will not be too deeply affected by the actions of

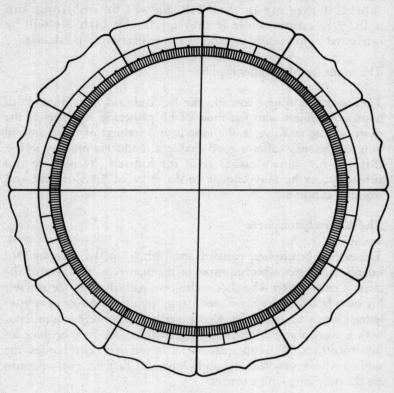

The Hemispheres

other people. He will be able to distance himself from those around him and also from public movements and events. He may keep his eye firmly fixed on the main chance, or on his own needs and feelings or on the needs of humanity in general, rather than to spend his energies on those who are around him. Such a person has a need to develop a career or a personal philosophy of life which fulfils him. If the planets are grouped in the 8th, 9th or 12th house, the subject will have strong spiritual needs and will see life in terms of related spiritual values. If they are in the 10th, he will be ambitious and politically astute, while if they are in the 11th, he will be interested in humanity in general and education in particular.

The lower (northern) hemisphere

The lower hemisphere contains the 1st, 2nd, 3rd, 4th, 5th and 6th houses. A subject who has most of his planets in this part of the chart will be sensitive to the moods and feelings of those around him and he may suffer a good deal as a result. He may try to live through his family rather than for himself, he may be too subjective or he may choose to do most of his thinking and working at home.

The eastern hemisphere

The eastern hemisphere contains the 10th, 11th, 1st, 2nd and 3rd houses. A subject who has most of his planets in this area of the chart is a self-starter who chooses his own path through life and sets his own boundaries. He is not happy living off other people or being kept by someone else. He has the burden of being an initiator both at work and in his personal life, as little is likely to be done for him by others. When the planets are in the first three houses, the subject is very self-absorbed and convinced that his own opinions are the only ones which matter.

The western hemisphere

The western hemisphere contains the 4th, 5th, 6th, 7th, 8th and 9th houses. A subject who has most of his planets in this area of the chart will need to be very diplomatic in order to keep those around him on his side. He may be looked after in some way by other people or he may spend his life supporting and motivating others. When the majority of planets are in the 6th, 7th and 8th houses he will use his energy to fulfil the needs of others. He may create a situation of being needed by bringing a number of children into the world to love and look after.

Planetary Features

The chart ruler

The chart ruler is the planet which rules the sign that is rising over the horizon at the time of birth. Therefore, if a subject has Gemini rising, his ruling planet will be Mercury. The sign and house which the ruling planet occupies is particularly important. Note the illustration below which shows Gemini rising.

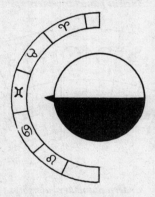

Gemini Rising (ruled by Mercury)

Ruling planets and their signs

☉	Sun	Leo
☽	Moon	Cancer
☿	Mercury	Gemini and Virgo
♀	Venus	Taurus and Libra
♂	Mars	Aries (in ancient astrology, also Scorpio)
♃	Jupiter	Sagittarius (in ancient astrology, also Pisces)
♄	Saturn	Capricorn (in ancient astrology, also Aquarius)
♅	Uranus	Aquarius
♆	Neptune	Pisces
♇	Pluto	Scorpio

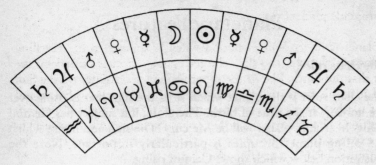

Ancient planetary rulerships

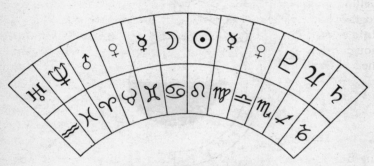

Modern planetary rulerships

The rising planet

The rising planet is the first one to appear after the ascendant. This usually means the first planet to be seen in the first house. If the first house is untenanted, then one must look at the second or third house. If there is nothing near the ascendant in the first and second house but there *is* a planet which is nearby in the twelfth house, then this is deemed to be the rising planet. My own chart is a good example of this because, technically speaking, my rising planet is Pluto which is in my third house at 7 degrees Leo but my Saturn is at 24 degrees of Gemini and my ascendant is 25 degrees of Gemini. Therefore, Saturn takes over as my rising planet.

Retrograde planets

A planet is in retrograde motion when it appears to be travelling backwards through the sky. The retrograde effect is caused by the fact that the Earth, like all the other planets, travels around the Sun and it is this juxtaposition between the motion of the Earth and that of the other planets which causes this apparent change in direction. The effect is rather like that experienced by a traveller in an express train who passes a slower commuter train. The commuter train is actually travelling in the same direction as the express train but from the passenger's point of view, it appears to be travelling *backwards*! Incidentally, the Sun and Moon are never retrograde but the nodes of the Moon are always retrograde.

In a natal chart a retrograde planet represents a weak point although this is less significant in the case of the impersonal distant planets of Uranus, Neptune and Pluto.

Billy Connolly's Chart

Using Billy Connolly's chart as an example, let us take a brief look at what we have so far. His chart has a well-spread bowl shape with a strong southern (upper) hemisphere and a strong eastern (left) hemisphere. This would suggest that Billy is comfortable in the public arena and that he is ambitious and hard-working. He is a self-starter with a strong sense of his own abilities and limitations. The groups of planets in the two houses which refer to money, goods and deeply-felt personal values are emphasized. This suggests that he seeks material security and also that he commits himself fully to any course of action which he undertakes. He is not overly self-absorbed and can fit into a group or a team quite happily when necessary.

Billy's Libran ascendant makes him sociable, less acerbic in private than on stage and also an excellent communicator. He is highly conscious of his image, both professionally and also as an ordinary person. He would hate to do anything which would make

BIRTH CHART

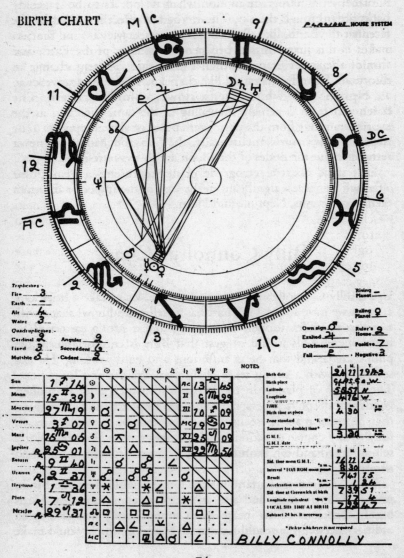

BILLY CONNOLLY

him look either dishonourable or ridiculous. His ruling planet, Venus, is opposed by Uranus, which suggests that he could be cheated by business partners, agents and so on. The romantic side of his life may be erratic, but he will be loved by the public for his eccentricity and his genius. His well-aspected Mercury in Scorpio makes him a sharp observer of people's foibles, probably a good mimic and also a very quick thinker, but he can be very sarcastic. In theory, his rising planet is Mars which gives him zest and energy, but Neptune in the twelfth house is much closer to the ascendant which will make him very imaginative, creative and able to bring his rich fantasy life to bear upon his job as an entertainer. This Neptune also suggests an inner sense of vulnerability and, along with Mars and Mercury in Scorpio and the eighth house stellium, indicates a need for caution and self protection. He could be offensive at times in order to protect himself. He feels a constant need both to prove and to improve himself. Billy has four planets which were retrograde at his birth — Jupiter, Saturn, Uranus and Pluto. There is rarely a problem when these outer planets are retrograde except in the case of Jupiter, which in Billy's case reinforces the fact that he could be too trusting over business and money matters. A retrograde Saturn suggests that he may have been over-disciplined as a child and that he will continue to impose a heavy weight of discipline upon himself throughout his life. Every writer and entertainer who makes good seems to have a strong or 'difficult' Saturn, which goes to show how important self-discipline is for such people.

A personal observation

Before leaving this chapter, I would like to pass on a personal observation or two. I am occasionally asked if people of one or two particular zodiac signs are more inclined to come for readings than others. Where private readings are concerned, an astrologer sees people of all signs of the zodiac more or less equally, but some signs will be represented more than others at any one time. The reason for this is quite simple. A group of planets moving around the ecliptic will affect one group of people adversely at one time and a different group at another time. However, when it comes to working at public exhibitions, the situation is quite different. By far the most common group of individuals coming for readings is Gemini, closely followed by Cancer and a significant number of Sagittarians and Pisceans. On many occasions I have found up to half the clients have been Gemini with perhaps another 25 percent being Cancer.

However, when we look at chart shaping, the situation shows considerable differences. By far the majority of private clients have personal planets (Sun, Moon, Mercury, Venus and Mars) grouped around the ascendant. These people are very intuitive and are often interested in New Age subjects. They are also very self-absorbed, very independent in their lifestyle and possibly rather eccentric. Many of them live alone, either because they do not find marriage conducive to their natures or because other people find them difficult to cope with. The ones who are actually married have partners who are happy to leave them to their own devices, possibly in exchange for financial security.

Quick Clues to the Hemispheres

Upper: Either interested in themselves or in wide-ranging issues but *not* in home life so much. Could need a sustaining career in public life.

Lower: Sensitive to moods and feelings of those around them. May work from home or be interested in home affairs.

Eastern: Self-starters, who motivate themselves and others but could be self-absorbed.

Western: People who can be diplomatic and whose lives require them to take others into consideration most of the time. They may live according to the needs and decisions of those around them rather than their own.

CHAPTER THREE

A BEGINNER'S GUIDE TO CHART WEIGHTING

As soon as a student of astrology learns to compile a chart (whether by hand or with the aid of a computer), he comes up against the knotty problem of interpretation. The glyphs and chart wheel on the page before him all look familiar enough but they don't speak to him in the same magical way that they do to an experienced astrologer. Reading books on astrology is essential to learning the subject, but there really is no substitute for actually doing practical examples. The following advice should help a beginner to cut some of the corners.

An exercise for beginners

The following method is one which I adopt when teaching absolute beginners because it doesn't even require you to erect a chart. I suggest you make several (enlarged) photocopies of the chart weighting form on page 79. Now look up each planet using an ephemeris. If you do not have an ephemeris and just want to practice, you could use the figures on the sample ephemeris on page 93. I suggest that you try to keep your writing small and neat because several planets may need to be placed in the same zodiac sign. It is a good idea to get used to using the planetary glyphs at this stage because this will save you valuable space in exercises like this one. As a reminder, they are as follows:

☉	Sun	♃	Jupiter
☽	Moon	♄	Saturn
☿	Mercury	♅	Uranus
♀	Venus	♆	Neptune
♂	Mars	♇	Pluto

Now make a note of the number of masculine and feminine planets, the number of planets in each element (fire, earth, air and water), and the number of planets in each quality (cardinal, fixed and mutable), and then fill in the totals in the boxes at the bottom of the form. Remember that there are ten planets in all, so the total for each group should be ten.

Once you have done all this, you can make a provisional interpretation based on the placement of the planets and their 'weighting'.

Masculine/feminine

More masculine planets than feminine ones: This suggests extroversion, confidence and assertiveness and the ability solve problems with courage and enterprise.

More feminine planets than masculine ones: This suggests introversion, shyness and passivity and the ability to nurture, conserve and to solve problems by intuitive means.

Remember that you haven't yet discovered the position of the ascendant and midheaven at this early stage, and that the masculine/feminine weighting may be altered when you have this further information. For example, a planetary weighting of six masculine and four feminine planets would change if both the ascendant and midheaven were in feminine signs.

Chart weighting form

	PLANET(S)	M/F	ELEMENT	QUALITY
♈ Aries		M	Fire	Cardinal
♉ Taurus		F	Earth	Fixed
♊ Gemini		M	Air	Mutable
♋ Cancer		F	Water	Cardinal
♌ Leo		M	Fire	Fixed
♍ Virgo		F	Earth	Mutable
♎ Libra		M	Air	Cardinal
♏ Scorpio		F	Water	Fixed
♐ Sagittarius		M	Fire	Mutable
♑ Capricorn		F	Earth	Cardinal
♒ Aquarius		M	Air	Fixed
♓ Pisces		F	Water	Mutable

Masculine	
Feminine	

Fire	
Earth	
Air	
Water	

Cardinal	
Fixed	
Mutable	

The elements

If the subject of your chart seems to lack a particular element, he may compensate for this lack in several ways. For example, he may be attracted to others who have this element in abundance, or he may behave in a way which is particularly associated with the missing element.

Mainly Fire : These subjects are energetic, enthusiastic and optimistic with a need to be in the centre of the action, making things happen. Fire people have a youthful outlook and a need to keep active. They are egotistical, headstrong and sometimes arrogant but can also be generous, warm-hearted and spontaneously kind, preferring to help others than than to take advantage of them. Such subjects can be independent and autocratic, they prefer to take control of their own lives and resist all interference or control by others even when this is well-meant. Quick to anger, sometimes extremely sarcastic and cutting but rarely sulky, Fire people need affection of grand scale. They have a good sense of balance between the material and spiritual sides of life. Fire subjects enjoy dealing with gadgets and new inventions.

Lacking Fire : Fearful or over-cautious, pessimistic and shy, these subjects lack enthusiasm, confidence and faith in the future. They may be mean and miserable, distrustful of others, sulky and surly. Other factors in the chart such as an ascendant and/or midheaven in the Fire element, planets in the 1st, 5th and 9th houses in addition to an emphasis on Cardinal signs will compensate for this lack.

Mainly Earth : These people are practical and cautious, sensible and capable, and are happier with concrete things than ideas. They move slowly and carry out their work in a thorough and unhurried manner, and their natural dexterity ensures that they rarely drop anything. Shrewd and careful, these subjects need material and emotional security and will put up with quite a lot in order to obtain it. Generous to those they love, but careful not to waste time or money they may appear mean to outsiders. They seek to conserve and protect both money and time in relation to their own lives and to the Earth in general. Shy, sensitive and tending to hang back in social situations, they fall in love slowly but are usually very loyal once they have pledged themselves.

Lacking Earth : A lack of common sense and practicality means that these subjects find it difficult to finish anything they start or even to do anything properly. They may be scatty, unrealistic and clumsy, hopeless with money and utterly unreliable. If the ascendant and/or midheaven are in Earth signs, or if there are planets in the 2nd, 6th and 10th houses as well as planets in Fixed signs, the lack of Earth will not be noticeable.

Mainly Air : These people are excellent communicators who are concerned with ideas and theories of all kinds. They seek answers to questions and then go on to teach and inform others. They are more tense than they appear at first sight, and may indeed live on their nerves. These subjects have many friends and acquaintances but they may not be particularly interested in family life. They love gadgets, especially those connected with communication, and their quick minds allow them to grasp the latest means and methods in our computer-aided modern world. They are capable of doing a number of things at once, are very imaginative and quick-witted but they can be verbally abrasive and sarcastic.

Lacking Air : These subjects lack imagination and lightness of touch. Their over-emphasis on practicalities and lack of a sense of humour can make them boring to be with. They find it difficult to communicate or to assimilate and explain ideas. If the ascendant and/or midheaven are in Air signs and there are planets in the 3rd, 7th and 11th houses together with some emphasis on Mutability, the effects of the deficiencies will not be as noticeable.

Mainly Water : These subjects are very emotional and they find it hard to look at anything dispassionately because everything is measured in terms of their feelings. Watery people respond slowly when asked a question and need time when required to grasp a new concept. Some Water subjects can be somewhat paranoid in outlook. Because they find it difficult to explain their feelings they can be quite difficult to live with, but as friends their kindness and sympathy is not to be missed. They need both to give and receive a lot of love and affection and will direct their affection towards family, close friends and also to animals.

Lacking Water : These subjects may lack intuition and be unable to see the needs of others. They may be too full of ideas or too fond of the material world to consider either their own spiritual needs or those of other people. They may find difficulty getting in touch with their emotions or coping with the emotions of others. If the ascendant and/or midheaven are in Water signs and if there are planets in the 4th, 8th and 12th houses the effects of this will not be so obvious.

The qualities

Although I have given the usual description of a person who lacks a particular quality, he may over-compensate for this and live as if that quality were strongly stressed. For example, a person with no Cardinality may be very self-motivated and a great initiator.

Mainly Cardinal : Cardinal people cannot be held under anyone's thumb and they need to take charge of their own world. Their energies may be directed towards themselves, their home and family or the wider world of work and politics, but wherever they are directed, it is difficult to direct their attention from their chosen course. Cardinality adds courage, initiative and self-motivation to any chart. It is hard to influence Cardinal subjects because they take their own decisions and believe that they know best.

Lacking Cardinality : Such subjects may feel that they are never in charge of their own lives but are manipulated by people and circumstances beyond their control. They may lack courage and initiative and may prefer others to make decisions for them. These deficiencies will be compensated for by an ascendant and/or midheaven in Cardinal signs and planets in the 1st, 4th, 7th and 10th houses. If there are planets in Fire and Air signs, the lack of Cardinality won't be so important.

Mainly Fixed : Fixed people have the strength and endurance to see things through and to uphold the status quo. They need stable homes, careers and partnerships, preferring to live within a known situation rather than to face uncertainty. Fixed people are loyal and dependable but can be very obstinate. They project an image of strength as an effective shield against their considerable vulnerability.

Lacking Fixedness : This subject cannot stick with anything or see anything through and he will tend to walk away from every problem. He may be easily bored or too busy chasing rainbows ever to make anything of himself and is good at starting things but not seeing them through to a satisfactory conclusion. His loyalties will fluctuate and fade and may lack common sense. If the ascendant and/or midheaven are in Fixed signs or if there are planets in the 2nd, 5th, 8th or 11th houses, in addition to planets in Earth signs, the effects of these deficiencies will not be noticeable.

Mainly Mutable : These people are adaptable, co-operative and friendly. They can fit in almost anywhere, put up with anything and turn any situation to their advantage. Mutable people can steer projects through periods of transition and can also bring them to a conclusion. Although gentle and likeable, these people seem to have more than their fair share of problems and can be selfish and ruthless when they feel threatened. These subjects may devote their lives to the care of others (or the care of animals) but they manage paradoxically to be surprisingly selfish at the same time.

Lacking Mutability : These people may be unable to adapt to any kind of change and are particularly unhappy when faced with uncertainty. They need lots of notice before they will commit themselves to anything. They lack flexibility and adaptability and may be far too fond of their own rigid and unchanging views. This will be completely altered by an ascendant and/or midheaven in Mutable signs plus planets in the 3rd, 6th, 9th and 12th houses, and if they have planets in Water signs this will make up for the lack of intuition.

Recent events in the Soviet Union offer an excellent example of the Cardinal/Fixed/Mutable states. The original revolution as perpetrated by revolutionaries such as Lenin, Trotsky and Kerensky was a *Cardinal* idea. The terrible stagnation carried on by Malenkov, Molotov, Brezniev, Andropov and Chernenko is typically *Fixed* behaviour, whereas the incredible ends and changes unleashed by Gorbachev are typically *Mutable* in style. It is also interesting to note that Gorbachev himself actually has his Sun in the Mutable sign of Pisces.

Quick clues to chart weighting

Gender

Masculine:	Extroversion, assertiveness, courage.
Feminine:	Introversion, shyness, nurturing instincts.

Element

Fire:	Energy, enthusiasm, faith in the future, youthful attitude, arrogance, impatience, the ability to have a go at anything.
Earth:	Practicality, common sense, capability, shrewdness, dullness, obstinacy, tenacity, laziness and a tendency to disregard other people's needs.
Air:	Intelligence, communicative ability, friendliness, quick-mindedness, tendency to be harsh and sarcastic or unfeeling at times.

Water: Intuitive, emotional, kind and sympathetic, broody, possibly unable to verbalize feelings, watchful and spiteful.

Quality

Cardinal: Decision-maker and initiator; has courage and will-power and will get his own way in the end.

Fixed: Stick with a situation, uphold the status quo, loyal and capable but too inflexible, hate to give in.

Mutable: Adaptable, versatile, can cope with changing situations but may lack perseverance, be manipulative, liars or very selfish.

Neil Kinnock's Chart

Now let us take a look at the weighting of Neil Kinnock's chart. Mr Kinnock was born and brought up in Wales, is married with a family and has a pleasant and rather gentle outer manner. He is the current leader of the British Labour party and may one day become Prime Minister. (I have not chosen Mr Kinnock's chart because of any political bias, it just seems to be a good example for us to look at.)

Gender

Neil has six planets plus the ascendant and the midheaven in masculine signs. This shows courage and leadership qualities. He also has four planets in feminine signs which shows sensitivity to the needs and feelings of others and also a measure of vulnerability

BIRTH CHART

PLACIDUS HOUSE SYSTEM

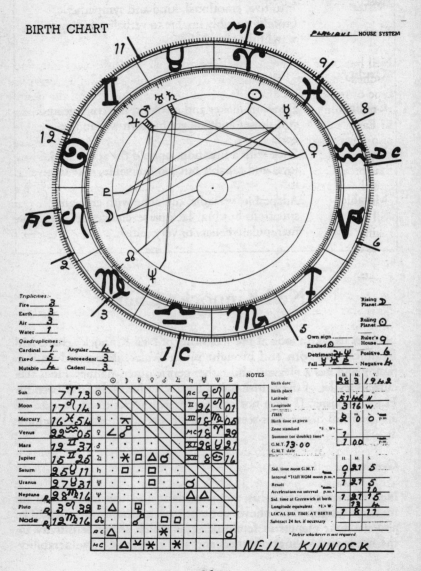

Triplicities:-
Fire __3__
Earth __3__
Air __3__
Water __1__

Quadruplicities:-
Cardinal __1__   Angular __4__
Fixed __5__   Succeedent __3__
Mutable __4__   Cadent __3__

Rising Planet ☽
Ruling Planet ☉
Own sign ____   Ruler's House 9
Exalted ☉   Positive 6
Detriment ☿♃   Negative 4
Fall ☿♃♇

	☉	☽	☿	♀	♂	♃	♄	♅	♆	♇			D.	M.	V.
Sun	7 ♈ 73	☉									AC	♌ 00	Birth date	28	3	1942
Moon	17 ♌ 14	☽									II	♍ 01	Birth place			
Mercury	16 ♓ 54	☿	K								III	♍ 05	Latitude	51	46	N
Venus	22 ♒ 05	♀	∠	☌							MC	♈ 29	Longitude	3	16	W
Mars	12 ♊ 37	♂	•	•	•						XI	♉ 21	*TIME:* Birth time as given	2	00	p.m.
Jupiter	15 ♊ 25	♃	*	□	△	☌					XII	♋ 16	Zone standard *E·W*			
Saturn	25 ♊ 11	♄	□	•	□	•							Summer (or double) time *	1		
Uranus	9 ♊ 37	♅	•	•	•	•	☌						G.M.T. 13·00	1	00	p.m.
Neptune	28 ♍ 16	♆	•	•	△	△	•	•					G.M.T. date			
Pluto	R 3 ♌ 39	♇	△	•	Q		•	•	•				Sid. time noon G.M.T.	0	37	5
Node	R 12 ♍ 16	☊	•	°	•	□	□	•					Interval *TO/FROM noon p.m.*	1		
		AC	△	•	•	•	*						Result	1	37	5
		MC	△	⚹	*	•	*					☌		Acceleration on interval p.m.			10

NOTES

Sid. time at Greenwich at birth — 1 | 37 | 15
Longitude equivalent *E·W* — 13 | 4
LOCAL SID. TIME AT BIRTH — 1 | 8 | 11
Subtract 24 hrs. if necessary —

Delete whichever is not required.

NEIL KINNOCK

and caution which helps to balance the rather overwhelming masculinity of the chart.

Elements

Neil has three planets in Fire signs together with the ascendant and midheaven in Fire. This suggests a very outgoing and rather assertive type of person who has faith and hope for the future and the desire to make something of himself and his policies. He has three planets in Earth signs which gives him practicality and common sense. He also has three planets in Air signs which gives him the intellect to keep up with a demanding job, to cope with ideas and to make sure that he is kept informed. Neil has only one planet in a Water sign and therefore he doesn't make decisions on an emotional level. If, for example, he gets angry about something, he doesn't react at once but will wait until he has calmed down and found out all the facts before taking action. However, the presence of some Water on the chart saves him from being unfeeling and uncaring.

Qualities

Neil has one planet in a Cardinal sign and also a Cardinal midheaven. Conventional astrological theory suggests that this prevents him from being an initiator, but with both the Sun and midheaven in Aries, I don't think he would lack initiative. Neil has five planets and his ascendant in Fixed signs and this makes him rather stubborn, able to 'hang in there' and reluctant to change for the sake of it. The fixedness plus the strong emphasis of Leo on his chart adds a sense of history and tradition to his rather masculine and forward-looking chart.

Neil has four planets in Mutable signs. This surprises me as it shows more flexibility than I had personally imagined a politician of his stature would have. However, I suppose a politician has to be flexible due to the changing circumstances and needs in the world that we inhabit. He must also be able to get on with all kinds of people and must have the breadth of mind and the sharp wits that Mutable signs impart.

Hemispheres etc.

Referring back to the subjects covered in the previous chapter, I suggest that we take a brief look at the rest of the chart shaping. Neil Kinnock's chart is quite spread out in a vague bowl shape but has the emphasis on the southern and eastern hemispheres as would be expected for any public figure. (Billy Connolly's chart is similar.) His Leo ascendant suggests that he is proud, honest and friendly but somewhat power-hungry. The Aries midheaven makes him want to do things his way and to be in charge, and the placement of his Sun close to the midheaven emphasizes this. Neil Kinnock is a born leader. The group of planets around the cusp of the 10th and 11th houses makes him hard-working, determined, patient and ambitious but also friendly to all manner of people, ready to learn at all stages of his life and able to detach himself emotionally when making decisions. The Moon and Pluto near the ascendant make him somewhat self-centred but also keen to help humanity and they show his concern to see his country prosper. Both the Moon and Pluto have associations with the public domain and the Moon is associated with home, country and patriotism. They also make him bossy and able to project emotion although, as we have seen, he is able to detach himself. He likes the sea and prefers his home to travelling around the world (Moon and Pluto near the ascendant), although he will always have to travel a lot in connection with his work (Sun in ninth house). On the strength of the weighting of the chart alone, he seems capable, sincere, ambitious and perfectly sensible.

CHAPTER FOUR

ERECTING A CHART

It takes a few days for a student to learn the mechanics of erecting a chart by hand and a further few weeks to become really familiar with the procedure. I taught myself to put a chart together with the aid of a book called *The Compleat Astrologer* by Derek and Julia Parker with a little help from a friend who knew the procedure. The book deviated a little from the methods which were commonly used by astrologers but it was quite easy to convert to standard astrology methods later on. If you need this kind of very basic information, I suggest that you get in touch with one of the astrological schools which you will find widely advertised in specialist magazines (e.g. *Prediction*) and find out what courses are on offer. You may be able to attend a series of classes in person or work with a tutor by correspondence. You may also be able to ask your friendly local astrologer to teach you, remembering of course to pay him for his time. This section on chart erection would be useful to someone who knows, more or less, how to erect a chart, but who needs to be reminded of the procedure.

I think it is important to learn how to erect a chart by hand and to understand the mechanics which are involved, but if you are at all serious about astrology it won't be long before you start setting up your charts on a computer. Practically any computer will do the job and there are a number of software houses which will be able to supply a suitable astrological program for any computer to which you have access. Again, you will find them advertised in the specialist journals. If you need to buy a second-hand computer, they may be able to assist you here as well. Astrology programs don't require much computer memory so you don't need to buy anything very sophisticated in order to run them. I still suggest that you get to grips with charting by hand before transferring to a computer, because it is only by doing the job yourself that you will know for sure which level of software you will need. It is worth remembering that even if you find you have bought the wrong type of software, most reputable firms will change it if you return it within a short time. They will also advise you of advances in development so that you can update your own software for a minimum charge when new products become available.

At this stage, I suggest that you buy a software package which will give you the following:

1. Lists of the planets in their signs and houses.
2. A chart wheel with a choice of house systems.
3. List of the aspects.

Later on you will want to include progressions and transits, midpoints, synastry, solar returns, etc.

Erecting a chart by hand

Gathering the information

Firstly, equip yourself with all that you will need. For example, you will need an ephemeris and a list of any time changes (for example, British Summer Time). You may also need an atlas, as well as a Raphael's ephemeris or the tables in books such as *The Compleat Astrologer* or *The Practical Astrologer*. Don't forget your chart forms and a few coloured pens.

You will need the following information for the subject of your chart:

1. The subject's name (maybe also address and phone number).
2. The date of birth.
3. The time of birth, plus a note of Daylight Saving, British Summer or Double Summer Time for that particular place of birth.
4. The place of birth, plus a note of the longitude and latitude.

The planets

At this stage you have a choice of approach because you could start by finding the ascendant and the house cusps or you could begin with the position of the planets. I personally prefer to begin by finding the position of the planets. I also prefer to use a midnight ephemeris.

A sample birthchart

The chart which I have chosen as an example is for a guy called Brian who was born towards the end of the Second World War in the London area. If you need another example of a simple London area birthchart, you will find one in my book *Rising Signs*.

The basic information needed to erect Brian's chart is as follows:

Name:	'Brian'
Date of birth:	7th August 1944
Place of birth:	Edgware, Middlesex, England
Time of birth:	7.30 a.m. British Summer Time.(Converts to 6.30 a.m. Greenwich MeanTime)

The ephemeris for August 1944 is shown over the page. It has been copied from the *World Ephemeris for the 20th Century, 1900 to 2000 at Midnight* which is published by Para Research of Gloucester,

Massachusetts. The columns are headed as follows:

Day	This is the date of birth
Sid. T.	This is the sidereal time
Sun–Pluto	The planets in their usual order
N. Node	This is the north node.

The position of the planets are shown in degrees and minutes, except for the Sun which is shown in degrees, minutes and seconds. For the purposes of this example, we can ignore the seconds in the Sun column. The signs of the zodiac are given in letter form in this particular ephemeris but other ephemerides show them in the symbolic form known as glyphs.

The ephemeris shows us the position of Brian's planets on the day of his birth as follows:

Sun	14°	20'	Leo
Moon	19°	1'	Pisces
Mercury	11°	27'	Virgo
Venus	25°	37'	Leo
Mars	16°	1'	Virgo
Jupiter	2°	29'	Virgo
Saturn	5°	55'	Cancer
Uranus	12°	23'	Gemini
Neptune	2°	15'	Libra
Pluto	8°	31'	Leo
North node	26°	35'	Cancer

At this point we have to make a little adjustment because these figures are for midnight, whereas Brian was born at 6.30 a.m. GMT. The most important planet to rectify is the Moon because it moves at a rate of roughly half a degree per hour. However, the 'personal' planets of Sun, Mercury, Venus and Mars are also worth adjusting if you want to do the job thoroughly.

The correct method of adjustment is by using logarithmic tables to convert each planet's daily movement into a logarithm and then add the logarithm of the difference between midnight and 6.30 a.m.

AUGUST 1944

Day	Sid. T.	Sun	Moon	Merc.	Venus	Mars	Jup.	Saturn	Uranus	Nept.	Pluto	N.Node
1	20:37:54	8Le36 18	21Sg36	4Vi 8	18Le14	12Vi16	1Vi13	5Cn14	12Ge10	2Li 6	8Le21	26Cn55
2	20:41:50	9 33 42	5Cp24	5 27	19 28	12 53	1 26	5 21	12 12	2 8	8 23	26 51
3	20:45:47	10 31 7	19 36	6 43	20 42	13 31	1 38	5 28	12 15	2 9	8 24	26 48
4	20:49:44	11 28 32	4Aq11	7 58	21 56	14 8	1 51	5 35	12 17	2 11	8 26	26 45
5	20:53:40	12 25 58	19 2	9 9	23 9	14 46	2 4	5 41	12 19	2 12	8 28	26 42
6	20:57:37	13 23 25	4Pi 1	10 20	24 23	15 23	2 16	5 48	12 21	2 14	8 30	26 39
7	21:01:34	14 20 54	19 1	11 27	25 37	16 1	2 29	5 55	12 23	2 15	8 31	26 35
8	21:05:30	15 18 23	3Ar52	12 33	26 51	16 39	2 42	6 1	12 25	2 17	8 33	26 32
9	21:09:26	16 15 54	18 24	13 35	28 5	17 16	2 54	6 8	12 27	2 19	8 35	26 29
10	21:13:23	17 13 27	2Ta45	14 35	29 19	17 54	3 7	6 15	12 29	2 20	8 37	26 26
11	21:17:20	18 11 0	16 40	15 33	0Vi33	18 32	3 20	6 21	12 31	2 22	8 38	26 23
12	21:21:16	19 8 36	0Ge12	16 27	1 47	19 10	3 33	6 28	12 33	2 24	8 40	26 20
13	21:25:13	20 6 13	13 24	17 18	3 1	19 48	3 45	6 34	12 35	2 26	8 42	26 16
14	21:29:9	21 3 51	26 16	18 6	4 15	20 26	3 58	6 41	12 36	2 27	8 44	26 13
15	21:33:6	22 1 31	8Cn53	18 51	5 29	21 4	4 11	6 47	12 38	2 29	8 45	26 10
16	21:37:2	22 59 12	21 16	19 32	6 43	21 42	4 24	6 53	12 40	2 31	8 47	26 7
17	21:40:59	23 56 55	3Le29	20 10	7 57	22 20	4 37	6 59	12 41	2 33	8 49	26 4
18	21:44:55	24 54 39	15 33	20 43	9 11	22 58	4 50	7 5	12 43	2 35	8 50	26 0
19	21:48:52	25 52 24	27 31	21 11	10 25	23 36	5 3	7 11	12 45	2 36	8 52	25 57
20	21:52:49	26 50 11	9Vi24	21 38	11 39	24 14	5 16	7 17	12 46	2 38	8 54	25 54
21	21:56:45	27 47 59	21 15	21 58	12 53	24 52	5 29	7 23	12 48	2 40	8 56	25 51
22	22:00:42	28 45 48	3Li 5	22 13	14 7	25 30	5 42	7 29	12 49	2 42	8 57	25 48
23	22:04:39	29 43 39	14 57	22 21	15 21	26 8	5 55	7 35	12 50	2 44	8 59	25 45
24	22:08:35	0Vi41 31	26 53	22 28R	16 35	26 47	6 8	7 41	12 52	2 46	9 1	25 41
25	22:12:31	1 39 24	8Sc58	22 27R	17 49	27 25	6 21	7 46	12 53	2 48	9 2	25 38
26	22:16:28	2 37 18	21 14	22 17	19 3	28 4	6 34	7 52	12 54	2 50	9 4	25 35
27	22:20:25	3 35 14	3Sg46	22 8	20 17	28 42	6 47	7 58	12 55	2 52	9 5	25 32
28	22:24:21	4 33 11	16 37	21 49	21 31	29 21	7 0	8 3	12 56	2 54	9 7	25 29
29	22:28:17	5 31 10	29 53	21 21	22 45	29 59	7 13	8 8	12 57	2 56	9 9	25 26
30	22:32:14	6 29 11	13Cp35	20 54	23 59	0Li38	7 26	8 14	12 58	2 58	9 10	25 22
31	22:36:11	7 27 11	27 45	20 17	25 13	1 16	7 39	8 19	12 59	3 0	9 12	25 19

8/23 Sun In Vir. 6:47   8/4 Full 12:40   8/11 3rd Qt. 2:52   8/18 New 20:25   8/26 1st Qt. 23:39

(remembering to *subtract* the logs of any retrograde planets rather than add them). If you feel you absolutely *must* achieve this quality of accuracy by hand, then I suggest that you take a course with one of the better astrological schools. If, however, like the majority of us you are happy to achieve reasonable accuracy by rule of thumb, I shall now demonstrate how to do this.

The Sun moves forward by just under one degree per day (about 57'30"), therefore a time of birth like Brian's which is just over a quarter of a day forward from midnight needs to have about 14' added.

The Moon *definitely* needs adjusting, even if you don't bother to adjust any of the other planets. It moves a half a degree per hour and therefore would have moved about 3° 15' from the position given in the midnight figures in the ephemeris to the time of Brian's birth at 6.30 a.m. GMT.

Mercury appears to vary its speed of movement according to whether it is in forward, stationary or retrograde motion and you will therefore need to look at the difference between the figures at midnight on the 7th and at midnight on the 8th and divide them roughly by four to find the correct motion for Brian's 6.30 a.m. birth. In this case, the answer is roughly 14'.

Venus is much the same as Mercury and in this case the time differential is 16'.

Mars is similar but the time differential here is roughly 9'.

If you only need a very rough and ready chart, or you haven't been given an accurate birth time, then don't bother with any of this. Simply move the Moon's position as near as you can to the correct time and write down all your figures as whole degree numbers, leaving the minutes out altogether. For example:

Sun	14°	Leo
Moon	23°	Pisces
Mercury	11°	Virgo
Venus	25°	Leo
Mars	16°	Virgo
Jupiter	2°	Virgo
Saturn	5°	Cancer

Uranus	12°	Gemini
Neptune	2°	Libra
Pluto	8°	Leo
North node	26°	Cancer

Finding the ascendant

This is the point at which you may be tempted to give up. If it really looks too difficult to work out by yourself, go and get help. It is also worth noting that my book *Rising Signs* gives another couple of examples with explanations for you to practise with.

Looking back at our example chart, we can remind ourselves that Brian was born at 7.30 a.m. BST on 7 August 1944 at Edgware, Middlesex (England). From this information you can proceed to calculate his ascendant by the following steps:

1. As Brian was born in what is effectively London, there is no need to make any adjustments for his place of birth.

2. Deduct one hour for BST. (The symbols h, m and s stand for hours, minutes and seconds.)

h m s

7.30.00

1.00.00

= 6.30.00

3. Look up the sidereal time (exact star time rather than calendar time) in your ephemeris. If you look at the sample pages overleaf, you will see the sidereal time is in the first column. The sidereal time at midnight on 7 August 1944 was 21h.01m.34s.

21.01.34

4. Add the birth time to the sidereal time at midnight. (Remember, there are 60 minutes to every hour and 60 seconds to every minute.)

21.01.34

+ 6.30.00

= 27.31.34

5. Now you will have to make an extra calculation which is called interval time. This means that you will have to add 10 seconds for every hour which you have already added, plus 5 seconds for every half hour. If you forget this, you will lose a little accuracy but it won't be a disaster. In this case the interval time would be one minute and five seconds.

27.31.34
- <u>01.05</u>

= <u>27.32.39</u>

6. The total time has now exceeded 24 hours, so we have to subtract 24 hours to bring the calculation back to the right day.

27.32.39
- <u>24.00.00</u>

= <u>3.32.39</u>

7. At this point you will have to look up the page for London ascendants in Raphael's Ephemeris (the relevant pages are reproduced overleaf). If you run your finger down (bearing in mind there are 6 columns on every page) to find the nearest figures to 3h 32m 39s you will hit a snag. The nearest figures are either 3h 30m 35s which gives an ascendant (the column headed *Ascen*) of 3° 45' of Virgo or 3h 34m 41s which gives an ascendant of 4° 28' of Virgo. Brian's exact sidereal time is located between these figures at roughly 4° Virgo. In fact when we check these figures using a computer, Brian's ascendant works out at 35° 56' Virgo which is, of course, very nearly 4°Virgo. (60' = 1°)

8. If you want to use the equal house system, all you need to do is to mark each of the house cusps at 3° 56' of each sign. However, if you want to use the Placidus system, you will have to turn to Raphael's Ephemeris again and choose the cusps which are nearest to the sidereal time which you have calculated. For example, if we took the first of the two Raphael's options for Brian of 3h 30m 35s and looked at the adjoining columns and their headings, we would find the following cusps:

1.   3°45'   Virgo

2.	24°	Virgo
3.	21°	Libra
4.	25°	Scorpio
5.	3°	Capricorn
6.	7°	Aquarius
7.	3° 45'	Pisces
8.	24°	Pisces
9.	21°	Aries
10.	25°	Taurus
11.	3°	Cancer
12.	7°	Leo

9. If the foregoing has puzzled you, get help, or get a computer!

Example chart, Brian

Let us take a look at Brian's chart in the light of what we have covered in this chapter alone. That means that we will confine ourselves to looking at the angles and the planets in their signs.

Brian's ascendant is in nervy Virgo, which suggests that he should be restless and clever and also able to focus his mind when he wants to. Health matters are important to him as is the kind of food he eats. He may or may not have problems with his skin or stomach. He could be a fuss-pot or a nit-picker, but would also be very kind, with a friendly and adaptable approach, a gentle unaggressive exterior and probably the famed Virgo sense of humour.

Brian's descendant is in Pisces which could lead him to marry a woman with an unusual personality who is frequently drunk and who never quite gets her life together! On the other hand, his wife could be kind, spiritual or religious in outlook and self sacrificial, especially where money is concerned. This is because the 7th house ruler, Neptune, is in the 2nd house.

Brian's midheaven is in Taurus which suggests that he wants to build something for the future. He would stick to a job and try to

TABLES OF HOUSES FOR LONDON, Latitude 51° 32′ N.

Sidereal Time H. M. S.	10 ♈	11 ♉	12 ♊	Ascen ♋		2 ♌	3 ♍
0 0 0	0	9	22	26	36	12	3
0 3 40	1	10	23	27	17	13	3
0 7 20	2	11	24	27	56	14	4
0 11 0	3	12	25	28	42	15	5
0 14 41	4	13	25	29	17	15	6
0 18 21	5	14	26	29	55	16	7
0 22 2	6	15	27	0♋34		17	8
0 25 42	7	16	28	1	14	18	8
0 29 23	8	17	29	1	55	18	9
0 33 4	9	18	29♋	2	33	19	10
0 36 45	10	19	1	3	14	20	11
0 40 26	11	20	1	3	54	20	12
0 44 8	12	21	2	4	33	21	13
0 47 50	13	22	3	5	12	22	14
0 51 32	14	23	4	5	52	23	15
0 55 14	15	24	5	6	30	23	15
0 58 57	16	25	6	7	9	24	16
1 2 40	17	26	7	7	50	25	17
1 6 23	18	27	7	8	30	26	18
1 10 7	19	28	8	9	9	27	19
1 13 51	20	29	9	9	48	27	19
1 17 35	21	♊	10	10	28	28	20
1 21 20	22	1	10	11	8	29	21
1 25 6	23	2	11	11	48	29	22
1 28 52	24	3	12	12	28	0♏	23
1 32 38	25	4	13	13	8	1	24
1 36 25	26	5	14	13	48	1	25
1 40 12	27	6	14	14	28	2	25
1 44 0	28	7	15	15	8	3	26
1 47 48	29	8	16	15	48	4	27
1 51 37	30	9	17	16	28	4	28

Sidereal Time H. M. S.	10 ♉	11 ♊	12 ♋	Ascen ♌		2 ♍	3 ♍
1 51 37	0	9	17	16	28	4	28
1 55 27	1	10	18	17	8	5	29
1 59 17	2	11	19	17	48	6	♎
2 3 8	3	12	19	18	28	7	1
2 6 59	4	13	20	19	9	8	2
2 10 51	5	14	21	19	49	9	2
2 14 44	6	15	22	20	29	9	3
2 18 37	7	16	22	21	10	10	4
2 22 31	8	17	23	21	51	11	5
2 26 25	9	18	24	22	32	11	6
2 30 20	10	19	25	23	14	12	7
2 34 16	11	20	25	23	55	13	8
2 38 13	12	21	26	24	36	14	8
2 42 10	13	22	27	25	17	15	10
2 46 8	14	23	28	25	58	15	11
2 50 7	15	24	29	26	40	16	12
2 54 7	16	25	29	27	22	17	12
2 58 7	17	26	♌	28	4	18	13
3 2 8	18	27	1	28	46	18	14
3 6 9	19	27	2	29	29	19	15
3 10 12	20	28	3	0♍12		20	16
3 14 15	21	29	3	0	54	21	17
3 18 19	22	♋	4	1	36	22	18
3 22 23	23	1	5	2	20	22	19
3 26 29	24	2	6	3	2	23	20
3 30 35	25	3	7	3	45	24	21
3 34 41	26	4	7	4	28	25	22
3 38 49	27	5	8	5	11	26	23
3 42 57	28	6	9	5	54	27	24
3 47 6	29	7	10	6	38	27	25
3 51 15	30	8	11	7	21	28	25

Sidereal Time H. M. S.	10 ♊	11 ♋	12 ♌	Ascen ♍		2 ♍	3 ♎
3 51 15	0	8	11	7	21	28	25
3 55 25	1	9	12	8	5	29	26
3 59 36	2	10	12	8	49	♎	27
4 3 48	3	10	13	9	33	1	28
4 8 0	4	11	14	10	17	2	29
4 12 13	5	12	15	11	2	2	♏
4 16 26	6	13	16	11	46	3	1
4 20 40	7	14	17	12	30	4	2
4 24 55	8	15	17	13	15	5	3
4 29 10	9	16	18	14	0	6	4
4 33 26	10	17	19	14	45	7	5
4 37 42	11	18	20	15	30	8	6
4 41 59	12	19	21	16	15	8	7
4 46 16	13	20	21	17	0	9	8
4 50 34	14	21	22	17	45	10	9
4 54 52	15	22	23	18	30	11	10
4 59 10	16	23	24	19	16	12	11
5 3 29	17	24	25	20	3	13	12
5 7 49	18	25	26	20	49	14	13
5 12 9	19	25	27	21	35	14	14
5 16 29	20	26	28	22	20	15	14
5 20 49	21	27	28	23	6	16	15
5 25 9	22	28	29	23	51	17	16
5 29 30	23	29	♍	24	37	18	17
5 33 51	24	♌	1	25	23	19	18
5 38 12	25	1	2	26	9	20	19
5 42 34	26	2	3	26	55	21	20
5 46 55	27	3	4	27	41	21	21
5 51 17	28	4	4	28	27	22	22
5 55 38	29	5	5	29	13	23	23
6 0 0	30	6	6	0♎0		24	24

Sidereal Time H. M. S.	10 ♋	11 ♌	12 ♍	Ascen ♎		2 ♎	3 ♏
6 0 0	0	6	6	0	24	24	24
6 4 22	1	7	7	0	47	25	25
6 8 43	2	8	8	1	33	26	26
6 13 5	3	9	9	2	19	27	27
6 17 26	4	10	10	3	5	27	28
6 21 48	5	11	10	3	51	28	29
6 26 9	6	12	11	4	37	29	♐
6 30 30	7	13	12	5	23	♏	1
6 34 51	8	14	13	6	9	1	2
6 39 11	9	15	14	6	55	2	3
6 43 31	10	16	15	7	40	2	4
6 47 51	11	16	16	8	26	3	4
6 52 11	12	17	16	9	12	4	5
6 56 31	13	18	17	9	58	5	6
7 0 50	14	19	18	10	43	6	7
7 5 8	15	20	19	11	28	7	8
7 9 26	16	21	20	12	14	8	9
7 13 44	17	22	21	12	59	8	10
7 18 1	18	23	22	13	45	9	11
7 22 18	19	24	23	14	30	10	12
7 26 34	20	25	24	15	15	11	13
7 30 50	21	26	25	16	0	12	14
7 35 5	22	27	25	16	45	13	15
7 39 20	23	28	26	17	30	13	16
7 43 34	24	29	27	18	15	14	17
7 47 47	25	♍	28	19	0	15	18
7 52 0	26	1	29	19	43	16	19
7 56 12	27	2	29♍	20	27	17	20
8 0 24	28	3	♎	21	11	18	20
8 4 35	29	4	1	21	56	18	21
8 8 45	30	5	2	22	40	19	22

Sidereal Time H. M. S.	10 ♌	11 ♍	12 ♎	Ascen ♎		2 ♏	3 ♐
8 8 45	0	5	2	22	40	19	22
8 12 54	1	5	3	23	24	20	23
8 17 3	2	6	3	24	7	21	24
8 21 11	3	7	4	24	50	22	25
8 25 19	4	8	5	25	34	23	26
8 29 26	5	9	6	26	18	23	27
8 33 31	6	10	7	27	1	24	28
8 37 37	7	11	8	27	44	25	29
8 41 41	8	12	8	28	26	26	♑
8 45 45	9	13	9	29	9	27	1
8 49 48	10	14	10	29	50	27	1
8 53 51	11	15	11	0♏32		28	2
8 57 52	12	16	12	1	15	29	3
9 1 53	13	17	12	1	58	♐	4
9 5 53	14	18	13	2	39	1	5
9 9 53	15	18	14	3	21	1	6
9 13 52	16	19	15	4	3	2	7
9 17 50	17	20	16	4	44	3	8
9 21 47	18	21	16	5	26	3	9
9 25 44	19	22	17	6	7	4	10
9 29 40	20	23	18	6	48	5	11
9 33 35	21	24	18	7	29	5	12
9 37 29	22	25	19	8	9	6	13
9 41 23	23	26	20	8	50	7	14
9 45 16	24	27	21	9	31	8	15
9 49 9	25	28	22	10	11	9	16
9 53 1	26	29	23	10	51	9	17
9 56 52	27	29♍	23	11	32	10	18
10 0 43	28	♎	24	12	11	11	19
10 4 33	29	1	25	12	53	12	20
10 8 23	30	2	26	13	33	13	20

Sidereal Time H. M. S.	10 ♍	11 ♎	12 ♎	Ascen ♏		2 ♐	3 ♑
10 8 23	0	2	26	13	33	13	20
10 12 12	1	3	26	14	13	14	21
10 16 0	2	4	27	14	53	15	22
10 19 48	3	5	28	15	33	15	23
10 23 35	4	5	29	16	13	16	24
10 27 22	5	6	29♎	16	52	17	25
10 31 8	6	7	♏	17	32	18	26
10 34 54	7	8	1	18	12	19	27
10 38 40	8	9	2	18	52	20	28
10 42 25	9	10	2	19	31	21	♒
10 46 9	10	11	3	20	11	21	♒
10 49 53	11	11	4	20	50	22	1
10 53 37	12	12	4	21	30	23	2
10 57 37	13	13	5	22	9	24	3
11 1 3	14	14	6	22	49	24	4
11 4 46	15	15	7	23	28	25	5
11 8 28	16	16	7	24	8	26	6
11 12 10	17	17	8	24	47	27	8
11 15 52	18	17	9	25	27	28	9
11 19 34	19	18	10	26	6	29	10
11 23 15	20	19	10	26	45	♑	♒
11 26 56	21	20	11	27	25	1	12
11 30 37	22	21	12	28	5	2	13
11 34 18	23	22	13	28	44	3	14
11 37 58	24	23	13	29	24	3	15
11 41 39	25	23	14	0♐3		4	16
11 45 19	26	24	15	0	43	5	17
11 48 49	27	25	15	1	23	6	18
11 52 40	28	26	16	2	2	7	19
11 56 20	29	27	17	2	43	7	20
12 0 0	30	27	17	3	23	8	21

TABLES OF HOUSES FOR LONDON, Latitude 51° 32' N.

Sidereal Time	10 ♎	11 ♎	12 ♏	Ascen ♐	2 ♑	3 ♒
H. M. S.	°	°	°	° °	°	°
12 0 0	0	27	17	3 23	8	21
12 3 40	1	28	18	4 4	9	23
12 7 20	2	29	19	4 45	10	24
12 11 0	3	♏	20	5 26	11	25
12 14 41	4	1	20	6 7	12	26
12 18 21	5	1	21	6 48	13	27
12 22 2	6	2	22	7 29	14	28
12 25 42	7	3	23	8 10	15	29
12 29 23	8	4	23	8 51	16	♓
12 33 4	9	5	24	9 33	17	2
12 36 45	10	6	25	10 15	18	3
12 40 26	11	6	25	10 57	19	4
12 44 8	12	7	26	11 40	20	6
12 47 50	13	8	27	12 22	21	7
12 51 32	14	9	28	13 4	22	7
12 55 14	15	10	28	13 47	23	8
12 58 57	16	11	29	14 30	24	10
13 2 40	17	11	♐	15 14	25	11
13 6 23	18	12	1	15 59	26	12
13 10 7	19	13	1	16 44	27	13
13 13 51	20	14	2	17 29	28	14
13 17 35	21	15	3	18 14	29	16
13 21 20	22	16	4	19 0	♑	17
13 25 6	23	16	4	19 45	1	18
13 28 52	24	17	5	20 31	2	20
13 32 38	25	18	6	21 18	4	21
13 36 25	26	19	7	22 6	5	22
13 40 12	27	20	7	22 54	6	23
13 44 0	28	21	8	23 42	7	25
13 47 48	29	21	9	24 31	8	26
13 51 37	30	22	10	25 20	9	27

Sidereal Time	10 ♏	11 ♏	12 ♐	Ascen ♐	2 ♑	3 ♓
H. M. S.	°	°	°	° °	°	°
13 51 37	0	22	10	25 20	9	27
13 55 27	1	23	11	26 10	11	28
13 59 36	2	24	11	27 0	12	♈
14 3 8	3	25	12	27 53	14	1
14 6 59	4	26	13	28 45	15	2
14 10 51	5	26	14	29 36	16	4
14 14 44	6	27	15	0 ♑ 29	18	5
14 18 37	7	28	15	1 23	19	6
14 22 31	8	29	16	2 18	20	8
14 26 25	9	♐	17	3 14	22	9
14 30 20	10	1	18	4 11	23	11
14 34 16	11	2	19	5 9	25	12
14 38 13	12	2	20	6 7	26	13
14 42 10	13	3	20	7 6	28	15
14 46 8	14	4	21	8 6	29	16
14 50 7	15	5	22	9 8	♓	17
14 54 7	16	6	23	10 11	2	18
14 58 7	17	7	24	11 15	4	19
15 2 8	18	8	25	12 20	6	21
15 6 9	19	9	26	13 27	8	22
15 10 12	20	9	27	14 35	9	23
15 14 15	21	10	27	15 44	11	24
15 18 19	22	11	28	16 52	13	26
15 22 23	23	12	29	18 2	14	27
15 26 29	24	13	♑	19 16	16	28
15 30 35	25	14	1	20 32	17	29
15 34 41	26	15	2	21 21	18	♉
15 38 49	27	16	3	23 23	21	2
15 42 57	28	17	4	24 4	22	3
15 47 6	29	18	5	25 51	24	4
15 51 15	30	18	6	27 9	25	6

Sidereal Time	10 ♐	11 ♐	12 ♑	Ascen ♑	2 ♓	3 ♉
H. M. S.	°	°	°	° °	°	°
15 51 15	0	18	6	27 9	25	6
15 55 25	1	19	7	28 42	28	7
15 59 36	2	20	8	0 ♒ 11	29	9
16 3 48	3	21	9	1 42	2	10
16 8 0	4	22	10	3 16	3	11
16 12 13	5	23	11	4 53	5	12
16 16 26	6	24	12	6 32	7	14
16 20 40	7	25	13	8 13	9	15
16 24 55	8	26	14	9 57	11	16
16 29 10	9	27	16	11 44	12	17
16 33 26	10	28	17	13 34	14	18
16 37 42	11	29	18	15 26	16	20
16 41 59	12	♑	19	17 20	18	22
16 46 16	13	1	20	19 18	20	22
16 50 34	14	2	21	21 21	22	23
16 54 52	15	3	22	23 29	23	25
16 59 10	16	4	24	25 36	25	26
17 3 29	17	5	25	27 46	27	27
17 7 49	18	6	26	0 ♓ 0	♈	29
17 12 9	19	7	27	2 19	2	29
17 16 29	20	8	29	4 40	2	♊
17 20 49	21	9	♒	7 2	3	1
17 25 9	22	10	1	9 26	5	2
17 29 30	23	11	3	11 54	7	3
17 33 51	24	12	4	14 24	8	5
17 38 12	25	13	5	17 0	10	6
17 42 34	26	14	7	19 33	11	7
17 46 55	27	15	8	22 0	13	8
17 51 17	28	16	10	24 40	14	9
17 55 38	29	17	12	27 10	16	10
18 0 0	30	18	13	30 0	17	11

Sidereal Time	10 ♑	11 ♑	12 ♒	Ascen ♈	2 ♉	3 ♊
H. M. S.	°	°	°	° °	°	°
18 0 0	0	18	13	0 17	17	11
18 4 22	1	20	14	2 39	19	13
18 8 43	2	21	16	5 19	20	14
18 13 5	3	22	17	7 55	22	15
18 17 26	4	23	19	10 29	23	16
18 21 48	5	24	20	13 2	25	17
18 26 9	6	25	22	15 36	26	18
18 30 30	7	26	23	18 6	28	19
18 34 51	8	27	25	20 34	29	20
18 39 11	9	29	27	22 59	♊	21
18 43 31	10	♒	28	25 22	2	22
18 47 51	11	1	♓	27 42	3	23
18 52 11	12	2	29	0 ♉ 0	4	25
18 56 31	13	3	2 ♈	2 13	5	26
19 0 50	14	4	4	4 24	6	26
19 5 8	15	6	6	6 30	8	27
19 9 26	16	7	8	8 36	9	28
19 13 44	17	8	10	10 40	10	29
19 18 1	18	9	12	12 39	11	♋
19 22 18	19	10	14	14 35	12	1
19 26 34	20	12	16	16 28	13	2
19 30 50	21	13	18	17 14	13	3
19 35 5	22	14	20	3	16	4
19 39 20	23	15	21	21 48	17	5
19 43 34	24	16	23	23 24	19	6
19 47 47	25	18	25	9 19	7	21
19 52 0	26	19	27	26 45	20	8
19 56 12	27	20	28	28 18	21	9
20 0 24	28	21	♈	29 52	22	10
20 4 35	29	23	1 ♊	1 19	23	11
20 8 45	30	24	4	2 45	24	12

Sidereal Time	10 ♓	11 ♈	12 ♉	Ascen ♋	2 ♌	3 ♌
H. M. S.	°	°	°	° °	°	°
22 8 23	0	3	20	4 38	20	8
22 12 12	1	4	21	5 28	21	8
22 16 0	2	6	23	6 17	22	9
22 19 48	3	7	24	7 5	23	10
22 23 35	4	8	25	7 53	23	11
22 27 22	5	9	26	8 42	24	12
22 31 8	6	10	28	9 29	25	13
22 34 54	7	12	29	10 16	26	14
22 38 40	8	13	♊	11 1	26	14
22 42 25	9	14	1	11 47	27	15
22 46 9	10	15	2	12 31	28	16
22 49 53	11	17	3	13 15	29	17
22 53 37	12	18	4	14 0	♍	18
22 57 20	13	19	5	14 45	1	19
23 1 3	14	20	6	15 28	1	19
23 4 46	15	21	7	16 11	2	20
23 8 28	16	23	8	16 54	3	21
23 12 10	17	24	9	17 37	4	22
23 15 52	18	25	10	18 20	4	23
23 19 34	19	26	11	19 2	5	24
23 23 15	20	27	12	19 45	6	25
23 26 56	21	28	13	20 26	6	25
23 30 37	22	♉	14	21 8	7	26
23 34 18	23	1	15	21 50	8	27
23 37 58	24	2	16	22 31	8	28
23 41 39	25	3	17	23 12	9	28
23 45 19	26	4	18	23 53	10	♎
23 49 0	27	5	19	24 33	10	♍
23 52 40	28	6	20	25 14	11	1
23 56 20	29	8	21	25 56	12	2
24 0 0	30	9	22	26 36	13	3

finish what he starts. He may be drawn to gardening, cooking or building work and would be stubborn and wilful about his aims and ambitions.

Brian's nadir is in Scorpio which suggests that he may be strongly attached to his family and possible bound in some way by the past. He should have an emotional need for security and mothering but may not always be able to express this as the nadir's ruler, Pluto, is in the 12th house. Traditional astrological thinking suggests that he came into the world at a bad time and will go out of it at an equally bad time.

Brian has the Sun in proud Leo and should therefore be fond of his family, generous and loving, but also arrogant, bossy and inclined to irritability and panicky feelings. Venus and Pluto are also in Leo, so the Leo need for drama and a feeling of importance is emphasized. Venus makes him seek a stable relationship but also makes him attractive to other women. Jupiter, Mercury and Mars are in Virgo, which adds to his nervousness and restlessness but also reinforced his inclination to work hard and to make money from Virgoan jobs. Mercury rules Virgo and is very comfortable there, so his mind should work very well. Saturn is in Cancer which may signify some kind of parental problem. Uranus in Gemini suggests an interrupted career together with an off-beat mind, while Neptune in Libra gives him a love of beauty and some inclination towards the values of the 1970s hippy generation. The Moon is very strong behind the handle of a bucket chart. This strong Moon is in Pisces, therefore his feelings may rule him and his intuition could be very strong. He is sensitive and vulnerable and may have strong religious or spiritual interests. Being on the cusp of the 7th and 8th houses, he needs to relate to and co-operate with other people, although the rest of the chart suggests that he may be rather self-orientated.

So how does this fit?

Brian was born in London when Hitler was busy dropping doodle-bugs. His father died suddenly when he was six, and his mother was a kindly but obsessive person who died while Brian was in his early

BIRTH CHART

PLACIDUS HOUSE SYSTEM

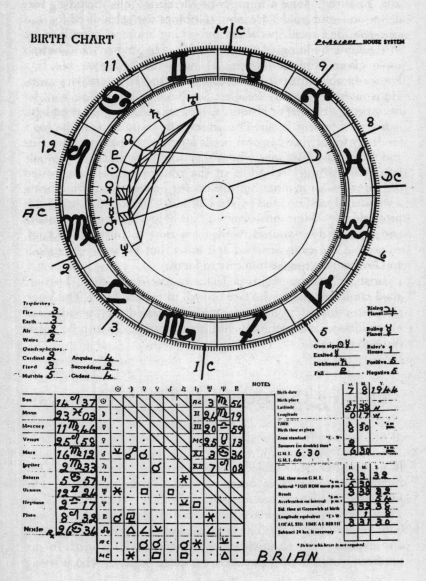

Trophicities:
- Fire ... 3
- Earth ... 3
- Air ... 3
- Water ... 2

Quadruplicities:
- Cardinal ... 2
- Fixed ... 3
- Mutable ... 5
- Angular ... 4
- Succeddent ... 2
- Cadent ... 4

- Rising Planet ... ♃
- Ruling Planet ... ♂
- Own sign ... ☿
- Exalted ... ♂
- Detriment ... ♄
- Fall ... ♇
- Ruler's House ... 1
- Positive ... 6
- Negative ... 6

	☉	☽	☿	♀	♂	♃	♄	♅	♆	♇	NOTES
Sun	14 ♌ 37	☉						AC	3 ♏ 56		
Moon	23 ♓ 03	☽						II	24 ♏ 19		
Mercury	11 ♏ 46							III	20 ♐ 59		
Venus	25 ♌ 58	☿		☌				MC	25 ♑ 13		
Mars	16 ♏ 19	☌			☌			XI	3 ♒ 36		
Jupiter	9 ♏ 33	♃			☌			XII	7 ♓ 08		
Saturn	5 ♋ 57	♄				☌	*				
Uranus	12 ♊ 24	♅	*	□	□						
Neptune	9 ♎ 17	♆			☌		□				
Pluto	8 ♌ 13	♇	☌	□	□			*			
Node	26 ♋ 34 ℞	☌	□	☍	*			∠	☌		
		AC		☌	☌	☌	*				
		MC	*	□	□	□			∆		

Birth date ... 7 8 1944
Birth place
Latitude ... 51 38 N
Longitude ... 0 17 W
TIME
Birth time as given ... 8 30
Zone standard *E·W·
Summer (or double) time*
G.M.T. ... 6·30
G.M.T. date

Sid. time noon G.M.T. ... 9 3 32
Interval +FOR noon p.m.*
Result
Acceleration on interval p.m.*
Sid. time at Greenwich at birth
Longitude equivalent *E·W·
LOCAL SID. TIME AT BIRTH
Subtract 24 hrs. if necessary

* Delete whichever is not required

BRIAN

20s. Brian has done a number of Mercurial jobs including taxi driver and tour guide. He now combines the roles of editor and salesman for a small specialized publishing house whose offices are in the same building as a radio station. His stomach and bowels have given him problems, as have his kidneys. He is a knowledgeable amateur historian and he speaks several languages. He is married to a very steadfast Scorpio lady called Roz who, far from being drunken or chaotic, is teetotal and very well organized. Roz does represent Brian's Piscean seventh house because she has a tendency to sacrifice her own needs for those of everyone else. Roz and Brian have two sons whom they love very much. The whole family is strongly religious in the traditional, old-fashioned orthodox Jewish manner but this doesn't prevent Brian from being a wonderful medium and psychic, although he doesn't practise this professionally. More prosaically, Brian enjoys gardening, cooking and a bit of do-it-yourself work from time to time. He is kind, vulnerable and easily irritated and upset, but his sense of humour and loving nature make him easy to forgive.

Brian, as you can see, is in fact very true to his chart. Leos are good family members who face up well to responsibility. The Virgo and Pisces sides of his nature are strongly stressed and the sadness of his childhood and problems with his education can also be traced through the chart.

Finding the ascendant for an overseas birth

If, unlike Brian, your subject was born overseas, you will have a few further steps to take in order to work out the ascendant. The following calculations are reproduced from my book *Rising Signs*. They refer to an imaginary person called James Smith who was born in New York City. The latter part of this section of the book also explains how to calculate the ascendant for a birth in the southern hemisphere. If you are a complete beginner who is trying to cope with this kind of calculation, you will need to take a few lessons from an astrologer in order to make sure that you fully understand the methods.

Example: James Smith. Born in New York City at 2.15 p.m. (14.15) on 10 January 1968.

1. Check that the date is correct because Americans sometimes reverse the day and the month so that 10.7.68 could be 7 October 1968!
2. Check for daylight saving. If you are going to do much of this kind of work, you will need a couple of books which are called *Time Changes in the World* and *Time Changes in the USA*. These can be obtained from specialist shops and dealers.
3. Look up the map reference for New York City.

Summary:

Date: 10.7.68
Daylight saving: Yes, one hour.
Map Refs: 40° 45' North, 74° 0' West.

Calculations

1. Note down the birth time in house, minutes and seconds.

14.15.00

2. Deduct 1 hour for daylight saving.

14.15.00
- 1.00.00
= 13.15.00

3. Convert the local mean time to GMT. New York uses a time zone which is 5 hours behind Greenwich, therefore add 5 hours.

13.15.00
+ 5.00.00
= 18.15.00

4. Look up the sidereal time in a midnight ephemeris for midnight (00.00) on 10.7.68.

19.11.55

5. Add the birth time to the sidereal time.

$$19.11.55$$
$$+ \underline{18.15.00}$$
$$= \underline{37.26.55}$$

6. Add 10 seconds for every hour which has been added, also 5 seconds for every half hour.

$$37.26.55$$
$$+ \underline{3.02}$$
$$= \underline{37.29.57}$$

7. Deduct the exact longitude from the new time. New York is 74° west of Greenwich, therefore the exact difference is 4 hours 56 minutes. This is based on 4 minutes for every degree of longitude.

$$37.29.57$$
$$- \underline{4.56.00}$$
$$= \underline{32.33.57}$$

8. The tables of houses are based on figures from 0 to 24 hours. Our sample figure is more than 24 hours; therefore we must deduct 24 hours and look up the resulting figure in the tables.

$$32.33.57$$
$$- \underline{24.00.00}$$
$$= \underline{8.33.57}$$

9. A book called *Raphael's Tables of Houses for Northern Latitudes* (or something which does the same thing) will be needed for this part of the calculation.

In my Raphael's Tables, the nearest figure to our result of 8.33.57 is 8.33.35. This few seconds difference is negligible, therefore we may safely conclude that James has an ascendant of 0 ° 20' Scorpio and a midheaven of 6° Leo.

Further complications

If James had been born at exactly the same map reference but *south* of the equator, he would have first seen the light of day at a place in Chile called the Archipelago de los Chonos. If that were the case, we would have to work out the calculations up to the end of step 8 and then *add* 12 hours and then *reverse* the signs. After looking up the ascendant and midheaven to give us the new southern latitude ascendant of 28° 46' Scorpio and a midheaven of 6° Leo.

All professional astrologers are familiar with this routine and, when exactitude is required, they will also fine tune the map references and correctly locate the planets for time of birth by means of logarithms. Computers reduce what was once a day's work calculating a chart into the work of a few minutes and they do it with perfect accuracy. But even when using a computer, remember to adjust the time differential — e.g. deduct any daylight saving and add or subtract to bring the time to GMT.

CHAPTER FIVE

THE PLANETS

The Sun

The Sun is a star, but astrologers tend to call everything in the Solar system a planet for the sake of convenience. The Sun is regarded as the first of the personal planets, representing the active, decision-making side of a subject's nature which, however diluted by other factors on a birthchart, is still one of the most dominant features of the personality. The Sun is associated with strength, personal achievement, leadership qualities, power and authority (or lack of it), and the need for the subject to express himself. It denotes adulthood and grown-up attitudes to life. It is concerned with creativity of all kinds, whether this be designing and building an object, a home, a business or a family. The Sun's placement also indicates how a person feels about creative endeavours and the experience of raising children especially the task of fatherhood. According to some astrologers, the Sun represents the father figure. It rules the fun side of life, such as holidays, pleasures, love affairs, games, some competitive sports and games of chance, important social events, and anything which allows the subject to shine. The Sun is intensely personal and is a strong pointer to the subject's modus operandi. The negative aspects of the Sun are arrogance, an inflated ego, bossiness, selfishness and an inability to see the needs of others. The Sun also rules the spine and the heart.

The time, and even the actual day, on which the Sun moves from one sign to the next varies from year to year which is why you will find variations between different astrological features in newspapers and publications. If your birthday is one of those which falls on the 'cusp' of a sign and you want to know for certain which sign is yours, consult the Sun sign guide on page 153 which shows the date and the time of each Sun sign change over the years.

The Moon

The Moon in not a planet but a satellite of the Earth, but for astrological purposes it is considered to be one of the personal planets. The position of the Moon in the natal chart reveals the inner feelings and underlying urges, together with attitudes learned by or instilled into a persona in childhood. It shows how the subject reacts to situations which are presented by others and how he behaves when his passions are aroused. Once again some of this instinctive behaviour reaches back into childhood or stems from childhood experiences. The Moon may have some karmic significance referring the subject back to previous life experiences. This underlying personality will reveal itself when a person is tired, ill or overwrought. The Moon's position shows the ability to adapt and also the subject's moods, obsessions and deepest needs. It also shows how the subject relates to the general public and the underlying mood of those around him. It is somewhat in tune with the collective unconscious but it is also intensely private and concerned with the subject's own particular unconscious. Traditional astrology ascribes the Moon's position and condition to the mother but we now see it as the subject's experience of being nurtured (or otherwise) by whoever took on this role in his life. The Moon's position can signify a subject's attitude to women (along with Venus) and his or her ability to nurture and care for others. It shows very basic needs and habits such as the kind of food a native chooses to eat and the way he eats it. One of the most important Lunar features is the way it refers to the subject's home and everything which is related to the domestic side of his life. Quite logically, when we think of the Lunar themes of home and mothering, the Moon's position shows the subject's experience of and requirements for security. The negative aspects of the Moon could lead to moodiness, a tendency to martyrdom, neurosis, lack of courage and leadership and too much dependency on others. Lunar negativity can lead to a clingy and over-demanding attitude in emotional situations. A negative Moon can, surprisingly, lead to the subject being a bully or a manipulator of others for his own benefit. On the other hand, it can simply suggest that the subject's mother has had a very difficult life and that she may be hard to get on with or that the subject's domestic circumstances are unsatisfactory. The Moon rules the breasts, thorax, lower lungs, stomach and some bodily fluids, as well as eating habits and food preferences.

Mercury

Mercury is another personal planet and it is concerned with communications of all kinds. These days, the 'winged messenger' may manifest himself in the form of a motorcycle courier, a fax machine or a phonecard. Mercury represents the ability to speak, write, to be understood and get messages across to others. Journalism, teaching, reading brochures and chatting with a neighbour all belong to the realm of Mercury. This planet rules the mentality; it refers to the speed, accuracy and depth of a subject's thinking processes and the ability to remember and utilize what one has learned. It is associated with schooling and basic education. More importantly perhaps, Mercury shows the kind of things a subject spends his time thinking about. Mercury is also involved with dexterity and hand/eye co-ordination, and its position and condition on a chart may shed some light on the subject of dyslexia. Although the literary aspect of Mercury is always the one which is stressed, it is also involved with mathematics and the ability to work out how many beans make five!

Mercury rules relationships with siblings such as brothers and sisters, and also cousins or those nearby children who have become like brothers and sisters to the subject. Mercury also rules neighbours, colleagues and regular participants in the subject's local scene. The planet also rules local travel and transport such as the subject's car, bike, local bus service and the kind of short journeys which he regularly makes. The negative aspect of Mercury could lead to too much talking and too little thinking, and an inability to communicate, learn or to impart knowledge to others. Immobility of the mind or body or a lack of clear direction in life can be shown by a difficult Mercury. Other problems may manifest themselves in a nasty uncaring tongue or mind. There may be unhappy relationships with siblings, neighbours or colleagues. Mercury rules the hands, arms and shoulders, upper respiratory tract and the nerves, as well as the skin, intestines and part of the bowel.

Venus

Venus is another personal planet and it rules open partnerships of all kinds, love relationships and the ability to put oneself into the shoes of others and to sympathize with them. It rules feelings of love, affection, companionship and harmony in all personal relationships. Because Venus rules open relationships, it concerns open enmity as well as love and affection, therefore this apparently loving planet also rules acts of war. Venus shows the way people feel about money and personal possessions, creature comforts and what is considered to be of value in a practical sense. Venus is concerned with sensual pleasures, feminine pastimes and attributes and the way the subject relates to women. It is also associated with the arts, social life and a subject's use of dress and grooming as well as the world of fashion and beauty in a wider sense. In a man's chart, the placement and condition of Venus will give a clue to the kind of woman he values, and what he wants from her. A negative Venus could lead to an inability to put oneself into the shoes of others or to form good relationships. A woman with a negative Venus may experience difficulty in accepting her own femininity, while a man with a negative Venus would find it hard to understand or like women. Such subjects of either sex may seek out partners who hurt or use them or make them feel inadequate. These people may become depressed about what they see as a lack of success in relationships or they may be clingy and demanding. Venus rules the throat, thyroid glands, lower teeth and lower jaw, and also the neck. It is also involved with some of the soft inner organs such as the pancreas, kidneys and bladder. Ailments connected with movement and spinal problems in the lumbar area can also come under the auspices of Venus.

Mars

Mars is last of the personal planets, and its position and condition shows how the principles of both action and desire are expressed. It shows the kind of projects which are chosen and how they are tackled. It is the adrenalin of the horoscope and it denotes the urge towards 'fight or flight' and the mode of attack when threatened. It generates a positive and energetic outlook to all things. Mars is concerned with sexuality, heated feelings and, to some extent, shows the things a subject does by instinct (along with the Moon, of course). Mars rules anger and violence either perpetrated by the subject or directed towards him. The negative side of Mars may make a subject aggressive, hasty, reckless and impulsive, or alternatively meek and lazy. Mars rules the head down as far as the lower jaw but the teeth, ears and bones of the head are also ruled by Saturn, so this can be rather difficult to sort out. Mars is associated with infections and accidents, especially burns, headaches, and problems with the circulatory, reproductive and urinary systems. Mars also rules incidents of violence.

Jupiter

Jupiter is the first of the transpersonal planets which is less associated with the self but more involved with interaction with others. Jupiter is concerned with expansion in every form, the acquisition of knowledge and the need to be free. Traditionally it rules religion and philosophy, the law, foreign travel, foreign countries and exploration. It also rules colleges and universities and all forms of higher education. All these ideas are related to expansion, pushing back boundaries, the gaining of knowledge and the freedom to utilize it. Jupiter is associated with deeply-held beliefs and the types of charities or enterprises to which we are drawn. Jupiter is supposed to bring luck, especially in relation to gambling or financial speculation. It is associated with the great outdoors, large animals and large ventures. Jupiter is also concerned with publishing, publicity and broadcasting. It can show, along with other planets, how a subject earns his living and the areas of life which he finds easy to cope with. It shoes the ability to co-operate with people in general and the urge to be charitable and humanitarian. It can describe areas where good deeds were done in previous lives and the actions and events which seem to be protected in this life. Negative Jupiter traits can give a subject an overbearing personality, turning him into someone who rides rough-shod over everyone or alternatively, into a greedy person who doesn't know when enough is enough. This can also denote a person with an over-expansive personality who has little self-control and may be a compulsive spender or gambler. Jupiter rules the liver, hips, thighs, the pituitary gland and some parts of the circulatory system.

Saturn

Saturn is the second of the transpersonal planets, therefore less involved with the self than with interaction with others. While Jupiter is the planet of expansion of horizons, Saturn is concerned with limitations and restrictions and is often called the teacher of the zodiac. Saturn rules serious thinking, attention to detail and doing things properly. It is also concerned with security, particularly of the financial and bricks-and-mortar kind and structure in every sense of the word. I have heard many people who, on acquiring a little astrological knowledge, have moaned about their particular Saturn, suggesting that it is responsible for all their problems, but this just isn't fair to poor old Saturn. Without a structure, a framework or a skeleton nothing would stand up straight, and without a measure of application and hard work nothing would be accomplished. People with a strong Saturn in their charts may well experience hard times, especially in childhood, but they are also self-disciplined, good at passing examinations and generally successful in life. This planet can show physical strength and endurance (or the lack of it), tenacity, emotional endurance, self discipline and trustworthiness. Saturn rules all those things which people don't much like doing, such as cleaning the oven, flossing one's teeth, doing homework, changing the oil in the car, getting up early and coping with pain. It also shows how a subject both overcomes problems and copes with limiting or difficult situations.

Saturn is traditionally associated with the father figure and the subject's early experiences of discipline and restriction of his wilder urges. It is the price one pays for too much self-indulgence. A well-placed Saturn can be found on the chart of someone who copes well with hardship and becomes a great achiever, possibly even an over-achiever. Saturn problems can make a subject austere, cold, unfeeling and too hard on other people who have softer personalities. A badly-placed Saturn can denote a lazy person who never gets anything off the ground, a subjects whose health is poor, a miser or simply a misery. Saturn rules the teeth, skin, bones, ears, gall-bladder, spleen, vagus nerves and the knees, and also the ailments of old age such as arthritis.

Uranus

Uranus is the first of the impersonal planets and rules detached relationships such as friendships and acquaintanceships. It denotes membership of clubs, societies, groups and political or humanitarian organizations, and is associated with modern inventions such as electricity, aviation, computers, television and the discovery of radiation (Uranium). It is concerned with the realms of ideas and the intellect and may be a bit too cold and logical in some ways. Most of all, this planet's role is to break down the established order and replace it with novel, experimental or idealistic regimes. It is a political planet which seeks to change and manoeuvre the world into new methods of thinking and being. A strong Uranus makes for an independent, friendly, kind but rather detached person with an inventive brain and a broad mind but who also has a strong streak of obstinacy and a determination to live life his own way. A badly-placed Uranus could make for an eccentric and rebellious person who seeks to make other people uncomfortable. A difficult Uranus may belong to a destructive or bullying type who cannot or will not compromise his views for anyone else. Uranus rules the ankles and the related circulatory system. It is also associated with nervous breakdowns and cramp.

Neptune

Neptune is another impersonal planet; it is so hard to understand that it is actually a difficult planet to describe. The positive side of Neptune leads to inspiration — truth, light and God-given wisdom. Neptune presides over artistry, music and illusion (the kind created by light, film and photography, colour, clothing and conjuring). It is also linked with religious miracles and mysticism of the mediumistic and psychic kind. It is associated with spontaneous kindness and charity, looking after those who cannot care for themselves, pity, and the desire to give hope to the hopeless. It rules hospitals, institutions, orphanages, mental homes, hospices, prisons or any form of real or imagined imprisonment. Neptune is concerned with states of altered consciousness such as mental illness, drug or drink-induced confusion and paranoia, as well as gases, anaesthetics, drugs and poisons. To be affected by a

Neptunian transit is to feel as if one is living on shifting sands with a new kind of reality being created. Neptune is associated with muddles, things which go missing in the post, deceptions, lies, confidence tricks and anything which is not what it seems to be. A well-placed Neptune brings the blessings of a creative imagination while its adverse side causes carelessness, impracticality, silliness, needless worrying and a tendency to live either in a fantasy world or under the influence of drink or drugs. Neptune rules the feet, allergic conditions and ailments caused by misuse of alcohol or drugs. It also governs some lung problems and generally nervous debility.

Pluto

Pluto is the last of the impersonal planets and is associated with transformation, regeneration and recycling. It rules major beginnings and endings including birth and death, sex and large sums of money. It is probably the most worrying of all the planets when one feels its influence transiting the birthchart. Pluto adds dynamism to the personality and its subjects tend to make sure that they get to where they want to be in life. It is also associated with endurance, the ability to change with changing circumstances and to recover from failure, illness or loss. It rules a strange set of situations, such as mining, things which are lost and found, surgery, butchery and the activities of the police. The ideas which underpin these points relate to those things which cannot be seen due to the fact that they are out of sight and have to be cut into or dug out; it also rules investigation on a more practical level such as detective work. Pluto is a violent planet which also has the power to heal or to transmute all that it touches. The god, Pluto, was reputed to be the richest of all gods, therefore Pluto rules wealth, especially that which is shared or co-operatively used and also the manipulation either of the self or of others by means of money (with a bit of help from Venus). Plutonic people have analytical minds and a flair for surgery, detection or big business. There is fear within this planet

and also the overcoming of frightening circumstances. Pluto rules
the reproductive organs, the unconscious and unusual situations
such as sudden and unexplained paralysis.

CHAPTER SIX

PLANETS IN SIGNS AND HOUSES

Each sign of the zodiac has its own character, and this will modify whatever is placed in it. Each house is concerned with a different area of life which will affect the goal, aim or final destination of that planet. Therefore, a highly energetic planet like Mars would be perfectionist and fussy if placed in Virgo or interested in travel and expansion if placed in Sagittarius. The same Mars, if placed in the 1st house would push the native towards self-development and the taking of a very personal road through life while, if it were in the 7th house, it would encourage him to co-operate with others and do their bidding.

The table below shows the association between each sign, house and planet:

Sign	House	Planet
Aries	1st house	Mars
Taurus	2nd house	Venus
Gemini	3rd house	Mercury
Cancer	4th house	The Moon
Leo	5th house	The Sun
Virgo	6th house	Mercury
Libra	7th house	Venus

Scorpio	8th house	Pluto (and Mars)
Sagittarius	9th house	Jupiter
Capricorn	10th house	Saturn
Aquarius	11th house	Uranus (and Saturn)
Pisces	12th house	Neptune (and Jupiter)

The houses

Here is a brief list of the kinds of things which are associated with each house:

1st house The self, possibly the appearance, the body, the ego. The start of anything.

2nd house Money and possessions, values and priorities. Growth of anything.

3rd house Communications, siblings, neighbours, neighbourhood matters, local travel and transport, education, day-to-day business matters.

4th house The home circumstances and the family, the mother or mother figure, caring for something or someone. Conservation. The beginning and end of life.

5th house Pleasures and leisure, holidays, games and gambling. Children. Creativity. Love affairs and sex for fun rather than a deep relationship.

6th house Work, duties and chores. Employers, employees and one's job. Health and well-being.

7th house Open relationships and partnerships. Open enemies. Agreements, treaties, war.

8th house Birth, death, beginnings and endings. Sexual relationships and deeply committed relationships of all kinds. Joint monies, taxes, legacies, corporate financial matters. Other people's values and priorities. The occult, psychic matters.

9th house Travel, foreigners and foreign countries. Large open spaces and large animals. Religion, the law and higher education. All things which seek to expand one's experience. Freedom.

10th house Aims and ambitions, direction in life. Status, one's career in the long-term sense.

11th house Detached relationships such as friends and acquaintances. Groups, clubs and societies, especially those which have a humane or charitable aim. Hopes and wishes.

12th house Mysticism, the occult, psychic matters. Being one's own worst enemy. Place of seclusion such as hospitals, prisons, institutions. Retreat and reflection. Self-sacrifice.

Remember, the sign modifies the feeling and behaviour of a planet while the house shows how it exerts its influence. The sign is what a planet *is*, while the house is what it *does*.

The Sun through the signs and houses

Aries Self-centred, impulsive, competitive. Keen on stability at work and at home but also restless. Highly-sexed. Can be sarcastic. Attracted to sports or large, military-type institutions.

1st Macho, self-centred type. Adventurous and courageous. Needs to have his own way. Can be successful in business because he doesn't stop to worry about other people's feelings.

Taurus Stable, confident, patient type who needs stable career and relationships. Materialistic, often successful in business. Conservative, shrewd. Attracted to the arts and dancing.

2nd An urge to accumulate money and possessions and also to live an easy and comfortable life. Could work in the arts or the beauty business. Sets own standards and priorities.

Gemini Bright, sociable, friendly, selfish. Highly intelligent and inquisitive. Easily bored. Good communicator. Hates being tied down, likes travel and novelty. Talented and dextrous.

3rd Needs to communicate, teach, write, talk and enquire. Uses intelligence and sharp tongue for good and ill. Needs variety and the chance to meet different people.

Cancer Cautious, conservative, down to earth. Also moody, spiteful, insecure. Clings to family, suspicious of outsiders. Tenacious, sensitive, a worrier. Good listener.

4th Seeks secure home life. Compensates for the love and attention which was missing in childhood. Clings to family and close friends. May work from home. Needs peace.

Leo Warm-hearted, generous, loving. Full of extravagant ideas which aren't always practical. Good organizer and homemaker. Won't be dominated, likes to rule. Creative. Good host and entertainer.

5th Needs creative outlet. May work with children or in something glamorous. Proud but generous personality. Kind but easily upset. Needs to feel important, and to be needed.

Virgo Meticulous and dutiful. Hates dirt or destructiveness. Good employee and also a good homemaker. Likes to work in business but not to be in complete charge. Sensible but fussy.

6th May work in health, healing, food and farming. Dutiful and reliable, good craftsman, meticulous worker. Modest but needs recognition. Formal, can't stand ridicule.

Libra Attractive, pleasant, good judicious mind. Likes to be in touch and up to date. Slow to make decisions but stick to them when he does so. Good diplomat but very selfish and can create own reality.

7th Needs company, may need good opinion of others. Co-operative, friendly, good negotiator and working partner. Attracted to music, fashion, beauty.

Scorpio Seems tough but lacks confidence. Strong likes and dislikes. Needs family backing and lots of love but may push others away. Tenacious, unforgiving. Can be very nasty but also very loyal and loving.

8th Attracted to world of finance, can deal honestly with other people's money or be an utter crook. Intense feelings about everything. May work in medical or forensic fields. Investigative mind.

Sagittarius Pleasant, cheerful, optimistic, sometimes unrealistic. Likes outdoor life and travel. May prefer animals to humans. Needs freedom and allows others to be free as well. Good communicator.

9th Drawn to travel, foreigners, education, the law, religion and publishing. Anything which expands one's mind or reaches the limits. Needs to teach and learn.

Capricorn Patient, realistic, responsible, hard worker. Dislikes rough, crude people. Ambitious and determined although often shy or weak as a youngster. Reaches happiness in later life.

10th Could achieve fame or infamy. Ambitious, materialistic and workaholic. Seeks public status but also needs secure and respectable family life. Wants own family to be successful.

Aquarius Unusual, eccentric, humane and kind. Intelligent and knowledgeable, good teacher, always ready to learn. Great friend but may be too detached and self-centred to live with.

11th May work for common good, drawn to group or co-operative enterprises. Uses mind but likes working with machinery. Good communicator, teacher, team leader. Unorthodox lifestyle preferred.

Pisces Idealistic, dreamy, kind, gentle. Likes travel and adventure. Needs secure partner and family life. Mystical, creative, artistic, self sacrificial. Can be haphazard. Likes children and animals.

12th Drawn to unworldly life but also money-minded. Could work in artistic or caring fields. Needs time alone to reflect but also needs love. Unambitious in the ordinary sense but wants to improve life for others.

The Moon through the signs and houses

Aries Quick thinker and talker but not good with details. Self-centred. Good worker but not so good at being a colleague.

1st Self-centred but also wants to help others. Gentle personality. Fond of travel. Prefers to work in feminine field.

Taurus Much common sense and practicality when dealing with everyday matters but emotionally quite unstable. Needs a garden or country life.

2nd Requires financial security and has a need to sort out inner needs and values. Attracted to the world of beauty or the arts.

Gemini Restless, loves travel. Clever and dextrous. Not keen on close emotional relationships and could be cool-hearted.

3rd Good teacher, craftsman, salesman. May avoid emotional commitment. Could be a liar or fantasizer. Uses intelligence and humour.

Cancer Moody, sensitive, intuitive. Close to home and family. Enjoys travel. Shrewd, possessive and clannish but very loving and kind.

4th Could work from home. Very attached to family and domestic life in compensation for love which was missing in childhood.

Leo Proud and self-centred. Loves children but cannot spend too much time with them. Ambitious, loving and generous but difficult.

5th Creative outlet necessary. Attracted to show business or working for the public. Interested in children.

Virgo Worrier, could be a fuss pot. Analytical, neat and clean. Drawn to teaching and writing. Difficult relationship with mother.

6th Could work in the field of health, secretarial work or service agency work of some kind. Literary. Possibly sick as a child.

Libra Logical, legal mind. Attracted to business or agency work. Needs friends and partners but can be moody and difficult. Refined.

7th Needs approval of others, seeks secure relationships but may have difficulty in getting this. Seeks variety in job.

Scorpio Could have lost parents in childhood or may have been ignored by them. Learned to keep feelings hidden. Emotions run deep and can be bad tempered.

8th Needs secure relationships. Drawn to big business, good with other people's money. Intuitive, has ESP. Sexual matters important.

Sagittarius Could live in a different country to that of parents. Loves travel, and needs personal freedom. Interested in spiritual matters. May have crazy relatives.

9th Good student who may have flair for languages. Will travel in connection with work and may emigrate. Interested in spiritual matters.

Capricorn Hard childhood due to adverse circumstances. Mother experienced poverty in her childhood. Has executive ability. Ambitious. Needs a well-ordered life.

10th Hard childhood with a strong mother who suffered herself. Wants success, status, power and will get this eventually. Public successes and failures.

Aquarius Independent, awkward and can be nasty at times. Needs successful creative outlet. Better with friends than family. Needs freedom. Has inner strength.

11th Interested in group achievements and activities. Good teacher and student. Changeable objectives in life. Could make use of sociability in public relations.

Pisces Mystical, sympathetic, kind, soft, vulnerable. Wants to heal the world and everyone in it. Artistic, talented but may not do much with it.

12th Secretive, mystical, mentally alert and very intuitive. May work in institutions. Has karmic need to improve life of others but may also be driven to spend time alone.

Mercury through the signs and houses

Aries Impulsive, quick-thinking, quick-witted, frank. Self-assertive. Can be sarcastic or lacking in concentration.

1st Concerned with self and projection of own ideas. Broad-minded, brain can be shrewd or intellectual.

Taurus More in tune with pictures or music than words. Sensible and cheerful, Rententive but rather inflexible mind.

2nd Financial ability, good bargainer, craftsman or salesman. Mind used for creating wealth.

Gemini Versatile, quick thinking, superficial, inventive and gossipy. Highly strung, nervous, good communicator and linguist. Easily bored.

3rd Interest in siblings or education. Talkative, can write.

Cancer Good memory, intuitive, opinionated, tenacious. Lives in the past. Kind, thoughtful, loyal. Dislikes change.

4th May work from home, studious, interested in the past and in history.

Leo Cheerful, optimistic, creative. Good public speaker, teacher, organizer. Over-optimistic, strong-minded. Arrogant, conceited and can be rude.

5th Likes children. Creative intellect and enjoys intellectual games. Poor at detail. Needs like-minded companion.

Virgo Analytical, shrewd, practical. Good specialist and problem-solver. Precise, organized. Good writer. May be self-critical or too talkative.

6th Interested in health and well-being. Good employer or employee.

Libra Romantic, tactful, gentle, artistic. Has good business sense but may miss opportunities through laziness. Sociable.

7th Seeks intellectual rapport with others, good partner.

Scorpio Sharp, critical mind. Needs financial security. Suspicious, possessive, vengeful and secretive but also loyal and steadfast. Shrewd and intuitive. Either utterly honest or a complete crook.

8th Good concentration and a good business mind. May deal with other people's money or the occult for a living.

Sagittarius Learns throughout life. Broad minded but lacking in concentration. Frank, versatile, restless, tactless. Loves travel, foreigners, sports. Interested in religion or philosophy.

9th Good student with a flair for languages. May work in the travel trade, broadcasting, education or religion.

Capricorn Rational, practical, careful, patient, serious. Can be depressive, or a stick-in-the-mud. Scientific or technical mind.

10th Career in communication. Good business sense.

Aquarius Inventive, intuitive, up-to-date. Good judge of human nature. May be unrealistic, insensitive, sarcastic.

11th Friendly, politically-minded. Could work in education.

Pisces Intuitive, imaginative, kind. Secretive, over-emotional and forgetful. Lacks confidence, gives way in arguments or loses temper. Flair for medicine, religion or entertainment.

12th Inward-looking, secretive. Attracted to mysticism and creative pursuits. Subjective, emotional, needs steady partner.

Venus through the signs and houses

Aries Strongly-sexed and affectionate. Needs lively social life and popularity. Creative, generous, high earner but big spender.

1st Uses looks to earn a living, interested in beauty and fashion. Image very important. Steady earner.

Taurus Loving and passionate, capable of deep emotions. Appreciates art and music. Good host or hostess.

2nd Shrewd. May collect valuables. Interested in arts as a business.

Gemini Flirtatious, light hearted, restless and fickle. May fall for a relative. Loves travel, music, art and drama. Adaptable but may never quite fit in.

3rd Sociable, friendly, gets on well with siblings. Can teach and study if inclined.

Cancer Affectionate and sympathetic. Leans on loved ones, clinging. Imaginative, home-loving, likes antiques.

4th Needs beautiful home and workplace. Extravagant.

Leo Needs to both adore and organize partner. Extravagant, generous, dramatic. Loves children and nice possessions. Needs to be appreciated.

5th Attracted to glamour, creativity, the arts and the stage. Flirtatious.

Virgo Critical. Possible disappointment in love. Restless. Good business abilities and communications skills.

6th Needs pleasant working conditions. May work in health and beauty fields.

Libra Gentle, lovable, refined, sympathetic. Good business sense but may be lazy. Fond of creature comforts. Image is important.

7th Could be lucky in partnerships. Needs good-looking partner. Affectionate. Shrewd.

Scorpio Possessive and manipulative. Sensual and passionate. Can either be cruel or very loving. Good money-making potential but could spoil things through pig-headedness.

8th May inherit. Sexual matters can be either a joy or a problem. Success may come through other people's money.

Sagittarius Freedom-loving and may marry late. Flirtatious, generous and idealistic but can be inconsiderate and thoughtless. Strong imagination may be used in career.

9th Good student. Travels abroad and may marry a foreigner

Capricorn Conventional marriage preferred. Undemonstrative, serious, controlled. Calculating; status and image important. Good commercial abilities. Needs steady job.

10th Happiness and success in career. May work in the arts. Diplomatic. Has influential colleagues.

Aquarius Needs freedom in marriage but may suffer. Detached, friendly but manipulative. Hates being smothered by love. Finds work in unusual fields.

11th Diplomatic, good fund-raiser. Seeks unusual career. Has influential friends.

Pisces Emotional, sentimental, mediumistic. Sacrifices all for love. Misunderstood. Generous or oddly penny-pinching. Needs creative outlet.

12th Attracted to occult and mysticism. May work or live in seclusion. Could have secret love affairs.

Mars through the signs and houses

Aries Aggressive, argumentative, self-assured, outspoken, impulsive, obstinate, independent and friendly. Takes initiative. Has mechanical ability and loves gadgets. May have headaches or eye strain.

1st Assertive, pioneering, forward-looking. Can be too impulsive and accident-prone. Strong, rather defiant personality. Hot-headed, selfish but kind.

Taurus Hard practical worker; a job started will be finished. Good singer or dancer. Smouldering temperament, stubborn and passionate. Has organizing ability and likes money. Sensitive throat.

2nd Money-maker and may be big spender. Competitive, domineering and acquisitive.

Gemini Clever and dextrous but rarely sustains effort. Talkative, restless, nervous. Accidents to shoulders and arms. Adaptable, needs job with travel and conversation.

3rd Keen at school and good at sports. Protective towards family. Argumentative and talkative.

Cancer Tenacious, ambitious, clinging, emotional, sensitive, sensuous. Needs security and family. Domesticated, good parent. Mediumistic, religious, patriotic. Weak stomach.

4th Works hard in the home, Likes carpentry or car maintenance. Can be quarrelsome at home.

Leo Enthusiastic, fearless, seeks leadership. Likes excitement and change. Can be overbearing. Sociable, affectionate. Has personal magnetism. May have back and heart trouble.

5th Keen on sport and games, a risk taker. Good with children and the young. May have love affairs. Likes leisure and pleasure.

Virgo Good worker who pays attention to detail. May be a busybody. Shrewd, critical, clever. Emotional life not easy. Suffers from skin and stomach problems when upset.

6th Hard worker, ambitious, critical. May be hard on self and/or subordinate. Inflammatory ailments likely.

Libra Perceptive, friendly, sociable, lazy. Good teamworker. Strong survival instinct. Flirtatious, sexual. Quarrelsome and may fail to learn from life. Bladder and kidney infections are possible.

7th Energetic attitude to marriage and partnerships but may be a quarrelsome partner or suffer disappointments. Lazy.

Scorpio Strong character. Works hard and aims high. Can be secretive, relentless, cruel. Perceptive, critical. Must learn self-discipline. Good detective or surgeon. May have reproductive problems or drink too much.

8th Attracted to medical, detective and insurance work. Sexy, jealous and conscience-ridden.

Sagittarius Boisterous, energetic, tactless, argumentative. Independent thinker, unconventional, sceptical. Has courage of convictions. Loves travel, adventure and sport. May chase opposite sex.

9th Active and interested in sport and travel. May take active interest in religious or philosophical matters. Woman may marry foreigner.

Capricorn Ambitious, power-seeking, obstinate, practical, self-reliant. Has executive and organizing ability. Can be cold, distant, irritable, unpleasant. Can't tolerate waste. Knees may be weak.

10th Hard, energetic worker. Can be ruthlessly ambitious. Will reach the top alone.

Aquarius Impulsive, intellectual, idealistic, impatient. Interested in good causes. Good in emergency but otherwise unpredictable. May be emotionally frustrated or frustrating. Weak ankles.

11th Enthusiastic and helpful but unpredictable. Likes clubs and societies.

Pisces Self-sacrificing, emotional, lacks drive and concentration. Penny-wise but pound foolish. Gentle, artistic, mediumistic, very creative. Successful when working on own projects. Has either very good or very bad feet.

12th Introverted, a dreamer, self-sacrificing. Attracted to the occult. Will work for the good of others or the world in general.

Jupiter through the signs and houses

Aries Freedom-loving, honest, courageous, extravagant and optimistic. Can be reckless, bullying or fanatical. Must learn to budget money and energy. Good entrepreneur, policeman, sportsman.

1st Broad-minded, cheerful and lucky. Has nice smile and diplomatic manner. May work in Jupiterian career. Must watch weight.

Taurus Loves comfort, rich living, good food and good company. Sound judgement, practical, reliable, good construction worker. May be possessive or over-indulgent. Traditional outlook.

2nd Lucky with money and generous but careless with possessions. Has spiritual rather than materialistic values.

Gemini Clever. Interested in teaching and communicating. Affable but unreliable. Mentally alert, versatile, open to unusual ideas and beliefs. Loves travel and literature. Inventive, restless, good agent or businessman.

3rd Gets on well with siblings. Interested in education and communications. May teach, write or broadcast for a living.

Cancer Kind, good humoured, protective, sympathetic, emotional and ambitious for self and family. Sociable, dutiful and patriotic. Can be possessive and touchy. Good business sense, especially good eye for antiques.

4th Good relationship with parents, likes home life. May buy property overseas. Could lack proper perspective.

Leo Big-hearted, generous, intelligent, loyal, popular, creative, dramatic, vital. Can be overbearing and pompous. Likes prestige and money. May work with the young. Flair for showbusiness,

5th Lucky gambler. Can make money from sports, creative work or drama. Good relationship with children.

Virgo Critical, matter-of-fact, kind, conscientious, ethical, analytical. May bottle up emotions. Success in medical or scientific field. Pernickety, absent-minded.

6th Enjoys work, interested in health. Could travel for a living. Spiritual rather than materialistic outlook.

Libra Sympathetic, kind, harmonious, charitable. Likes working partnerships. Can be lazy and self indulgent. Loves art and culture. Needs companionship, also needs praise and approval.

7th Excellent business partnerships. Marriage either very good or bad. Attracted to people with interesting minds.

Scorpio Shrewd, ambitious, strong-willed. Can be proud, conceited or over-dramatic. Loves a challenge. Interested in the occult, hidden things, mysteries, detective work.

8th Could receive an inheritance. May be involved with life-and-death matters of work in the field of police or legal activities.

Sagittarius Optimistic, forward-thinking, philanthropic. Could work in the law or the church. Loves travel and foreigners, animals and the outdoors. Needs encouragement and inspiration from others.

9th Loves travel and foreigners. Could teach or lecture. Self-opinionated, optimistic but tactless.

Capricorn Resourceful, responsible, capable and sensible. Can be penny-wise but pound-foolish. Thoughtful, reticent, productive, reliable. May be egotistical, unsociable, cold.

10th Successful career with financial benefit. Needs variety. Could be overpowering or over-dramatic.

Aquarius Humanitarian, impartial, imaginative. Can be tactless and unpredictable. High-minded, idealistic, fair, lofty. Scientific mind, good with new techniques. May do a variety of jobs. Interested in astrology or mysticism.

11th Many friends. Casual attitude. High-minded, keen on education and may teach. Spiritual rather than materialistic. Eccentric.

Pisces Intuitive, imaginative, artistic, humane, kind, romantic. Interested in medical profession, chiropody or fishing. Mediumistic, interested in mysteries. Needs a definite goal.

12th Some part of work is carried out alone. Interested in writing, publishing and also dancing. Likes the sea. May work in medicine.

Saturn through the signs and houses

Aries Ambitious, determined, self-reliant. Can be destructive, defiant, impatient. Has mechanical ability.

1st Inhibited, shy, responsible and serious. Poor health is likely. Happier when older.

Taurus Patient, cautious, methodical, frugal, stubborn, persevering. Works well under pressure. Materialistic.

2nd Works hard to make money and success is inevitable but hard-won. Can be possessive.

Gemini Logical, conscientious, shy, serious, intellectual. Unsuccessful in early education but is a late developer. Good at science, craftwork, computing or mathematics.

3rd Hard early life and poor schooling. Success comes later through own efforts. Helps brothers and sisters.

Cancer Shrewd, ambitious, hard-working. Homeloving, emotionally controlled, can be melancholy, self-absorbed, suspicious.

4th Deprived and unhappy early life. Could have had restrictive and unpleasant childhood experiences. May own valuable property later in life.

Leo Self-assured, good organizer, ambitious, hypocritical, anxious, jealous. Difficulty in having or dealing with children.

5th Joyless childhood. Difficulty in bearing or dealing with children. Successful craftworker or entertainer later in life.

Virgo Serious, methodical, prudent and tidy. Can be fault-finding. High personal standards, discrete, practical, Suppressed emotions.

6th Hard worker but may not enjoy work. Good craftworker. Responsible attitude. May suffer from chronic illness.

Libra Lonely if partnerships fail. Kind, pleasant, good judgement. Can be intolerant and impractical. May be very successful later in life, possibly through a relationship with a partner.

7th Later marriage with age difference. Faithful. Frustrated, restricted. May gain and lose through partnerships.

Scorpio Resilient with good executive ability but ruthless. Inflexible, serious, shrewd, jealous. Needs emotional release.

8th Careful, responsible attitude, especially to other people's money. Can have sexual problems or be morbid.

Sagittarius Dignified, prudent, fearless, forward-looking. Seeks higher education and meaning to life. Religious, intellectual. May be oppressed or be an oppressor of others.

9th Deep thinker and happy when older. May travel or deal with foreigners for work. Traditional religious outlook.

Capricorn Methodical, hard-working, disciplined, ambitious. Advances slowly in life. Can be selfish, mean, pessimistic and a worrier.

10th Ambitious, workaholic, reaches the top and then feels lonely. Obligations weigh heavily.

Aquarius Independent, original thinker. Aims high, reaches objectives but then changes direction. Scientific mind.

11th Too busy with work to make friends but loyal to those he has. Ambitious, scientific, humanitarian.

Pisces Interested in medical and religious fields. Idealistic, romantic, imaginative. Can cause self-undoing through over-emotionalism.

12th Sadness and withdrawal due to inability to express thoughts. Own worst enemy.

Uranus through the houses

Note

The outer 'impersonal' planets remain so long in each sign that they exert a generational influence; however the house placements do affect the individual chart.

1st Intelligent, unpredictable, individualistic. Modern scientific mind. Rebellious and possibly antisocial.

2nd Unpredictable income, may win or lose on a grand scale. Variety in career interests.

3rd Unusual education, possibly frequent changes of school. Lively mind, unorthodox thinker.

4th Unstable early life. May be unstable or disruptive.

5th Lively intelligent mind. May gamble. Will have clever children. May indulge in unusual love-affairs.

6th Unpredictable at work, could have two jobs at once. May have unusual illnesses. May do voluntary health work.

7th Unusual and very free marriage needed. Must have mental rapport with personal or business partner.

8th Unusual ideas regarding money, work and sex. May lose or gain money through working partnerships. May be morbid or peculiar about life and death.

9th Sudden journeys, may emigrate on the spur of the moment. Unpredictable life; may be both lucky and unlucky. Accident prone. Unusual outlook.

10th Sudden changes in career or direction in life. Far-sighted, dislikes routine. Leadership qualities.

11th Likes societies and clubs and has many friends. Interested in novel ideas, especially astrology. Humanitarian and a good teacher.

12th Secretive and may harbour odd ideas and feelings. Eccentric. Interested in astrology and the occult. Psychic.

Neptune through the houses

1st Dreamy, sensitive, artistic, impractical and forgetful. Unselfish, kind. May be a fantasizer.

2nd Likes artistic and aesthetic objects. May succeed in shipping or other unusual career. Otherwise muddled over money and possessions. Spiritual rather than materialistic.

3rd Intuitive and imaginative but lacks concentration. Good actor, inspired arts or music teacher. Something peculiar about brothers and sisters.

4th Loves home but may be disorganized. Imaginative. Early life may have been unusual but parents were kind. Animal lover.

5th Escapist, fond of dancing and untamed countryside. Creative and can inspire others. Kind to children.

6th Drawn to work in caring fields. Self-sacrificing and kind but can be impractical and unreliable in work. Strange allergic ailments.

7th A confused and difficult marriage. Must go own way but needs partner. May become a reformer or helper of 'lame ducks'.

8th Incapable of handling money. Can squander inheritance or be done out of one by others. Intuitive, imaginative, psychic.

9th Inspired. Could work in religion, philosophy, spiritualism. Travel over water important. May work on the sea.

10th Idealistic. Values are spiritual rather than material. May work in caring or psychic fields or may never work at all.

11th Idealistic, artistic and intellectual. May be inspired and helped by friends or betrayed by them.

12th Animal lover. Interested in poetry, art, ballet, music. Helpful and kind but impractical and dreamy.

Pluto through the houses

1st Dynamic, charismatic personality. Attracted to big business, politics and power. Life goes in phases. Brooding, hot-tempered, manipulative personality. Great powers of recovery.

2nd Grasp of business and financial affairs. Deep need for security. Manipulative and possessive.

3rd Terrific powers of concentration. May be influential communicator. Ups and downs mentally. May work with brothers and sisters.

4th Deep feelings about home and family. Domineering and fond of own point of view.

5th Can earn money from arts, theatre, gambling. Lots of love affairs. Strange ideas about children.

6th Tense, hard-worker. May work in investigative or mediumistic field. Will serve the needs of others but could make too much of a meal of this. Unusual health problems.

7th Good business partner but too overbearing in marriage. Intense feelings, especially about sex.

8th Intuitive, clever businessman. May work for community. Strong feelings, especially regarding sex.

9th May be bound up with foreigners or overseas business. Forceful personality.

10th Interested in money, business and politics. Powerful urge to rule. May have obsessive personality. Dynamic and successful.

11th Friendly, with a liking for clubs, societies and political organizations. May want to change the world for the better. May strive for some form of astrological or religious truth.

12th Hidden feelings and hidden obsessions. May have secret love affairs or a secret cache of money. Could be manipulative. May be completely disorganized but equally well-balanced and likeable.

CHAPTER SEVEN

ASPECTS, ANGLES AND HOUSES

Aspects

The aspects are the angles which the planets make to each other, and also to the ascendant, midheaven, descendant and nadir. Some of these make life easier for the subject while others denote stressful or awkward points which will need to be worked at. However, even difficult aspects can be made use of if they are understood. When looking at aspects, you will have to take into account the nature of the planets which are involved, the nature of the aspect itself and also the signs and houses in which they occur. Opinion as to the size of the orb between planets in aspect varies between one astrologer to another. I suggest that an orb of about eight degrees is suitable for the major aspects while one of about four is more suitable for the medium ones. Some aspects, such as an aspect to the nodes, need to be exact in order to count.

The major aspects

The conjunction ☌

This is where two planets (or a planet and the ascendant etc.) are within 8° of one another. The planets may both be in the same sign, which intensifies the aspect, or in adjacent signs which weakens it a little. This can be beneficial or difficult upon the planets concerned. For instance, a Sun/Venus conjunction would confirm beauty and a pleasant manner, while a Sun/Uranus conjunction in Taurus in the 8th house (as in Saddam Hussein's chart) is capable of inflicting suffering as a result of an uncertain temper and unpredictability.

The sextile ✶

A sextile occurs when two planets or features are 60° apart. Sextiles are traditionally supposed to allow the planets concerned to work easily with one another and can be an indication of talent or the ability to communicate ideas.

The square ☐

A square occurs when two planets or features are 90° apart. This is supposed to be a tense or difficult aspect but it can be the spur to great achievement if used constructively.

The trine △

A trine occurs when two planets or features are 120° apart. This allows the planets to work easily with each other and can suggest artistic or creative talent.

The opposition ☍

An opposition occurs when two planets are more or less opposite each other (180°). This shows some sense of frustration or difficulty especially in dealing with other people or in integrating different sides of the personality. An opposition between the Sun and the Moon can be especially awkward.

Medium quality aspects

The semi-sextile ⊻

The semi-sextile was once considered to be an easy or comfortable aspect because it comprises a half of the pleasant sextile (30°). However, two planets in adjacent signs mean that they are in signs of different elements and qualities and therefore may be at odds with each other. For example, a planet in the Fixed/Earth sign of Taurus would act very differently from one next door in the Mutable/Air sign of Gemini.

The inconjunct or quincunx ⊼

This occurs when two planets are five signs apart (150°) and it can be very awkward to live with. A **double inconjunct** is when one planet is inconjunct two planets at once.

Minor aspects

The semi-square ∠

This is a 45° angle and is supposed to indicate somewhat difficult circumstances.

The sesquiquadrate ⊡

The sesquiquadrate is 135° and is a pointer to somewhat stressful conditions.

The quintile and bi-quintile   Q, BC

The quintile (72°) and bi-quintile (144°) are supposed to show talent and vaguely fortunate circumstances.

The parallel ||

This is when planets are exactly the same distance above and below the ascendant from each other. This is supposed to act rather like a conjunction.

There are other minor aspects but they are even more involved and really aren't worth worrying about here.

Angles

The ascendant (Asc)

The ascendant is the degree of the sign which is rising up over the horizon at the time of birth. The ascendant shows how a subject presents himself to the world and it may have a strong influence on his appearance. It shows the kind of programming he received in childhood and may have a bearing on how he chooses to earn his living. The first house rules the physical body and may have a bearing on the health of the subject it also shows how the subject affects his environment. Planets near the ascendant throw light on childhood circumstances and are a very strong influence on the subject's outlook and behaviour. The ascendant can be a very strong influence on a subject's life but it can also be buried among other stronger influences. (Nothing is cut-and-dried in astrology!)

The descendent (Dsc)

This is supposed to describe the kind of partner with whom the subject chooses to live; however, it also describes the kinds of friends and associates with whom the subject feels most comfortable. For instance, a person whose descendant is in Capricorn will be attracted in general to those who are competent, serious, witty, subtle, hard-working and sensible. He won't feel comfortable with anyone who might cause him embarrassment.

The midheaven (MC)

This is traditionally supposed to indicate the subject's choice of career, but I have found that it also denotes his aims and aspirations in a much wider sense. For example, an Aquarian midheaven would lead to a desire to help humanity while a Cancerian one may lead the subject to surround himself by children and animals. The midheaven shows the direction in which the subject wishes to go and the kind of obituary he would be proud to have. Planets near the midheaven can show the kind of career the subject chooses and his chances of public acclaim and approval. The midheaven can in some cases suggest the type of partner the subject wishes to have to live with, especially if his aims, aspirations and lifestyle are as important as his feelings.

The nadir (IC)

This refers to the subject's roots and the circumstances which applied while he was young and towards the end of his life. It also denotes his parents and parental home as well as his own domestic circumstances. A major planet or a stellium on the nadir can indicate a severe lack of love or feelings of loneliness in childhood.

Houses

Angular houses

Angular houses are those which immediately follow the ascendant, descendant, midheaven or nadir. These are the 1st, 4th, 7th and 10th houses. Planets in these houses have a strong influence and may compensate for a lack of Cardinality, strength, courage or enthusiasm in the chart.

Succedent houses

These are 2nd, 5th, 8th and 11th houses. The 2nd house refers to the subject's personal resources (money, goods etc.) while the 8th denotes either shared resources or those of others which may have a bearing on his life in some way. The 5th house is concerned with creativity, even in the sense of creating a child or a family. It is also concerned with personal fun and leisure pursuits. The 11th house is associated with developing other people's creativity and creating anything which is good for the world in general.

Cadent houses

These are 3rd, 6th, 9th and 12th houses. They were once considered to be the dustbin of the zodiac or the places where nothing useful happened, but along came Michel Gauquelin and now all that has changed! Planets in cadent houses, especially the 9th and 12th, have a great deal to do with talents and aptitudes which have grown out of a subject's basic nature. (Remember all those *Martial* military leaders and *Saturnine* scientists.) The 3rd and 9th houses show how we learn and communicate with others, the 9th and 12th determine what we believe in, while the 6th suggests the kind of relationships we have with employers and employees, as well as indicating matters of health.

CHAPTER EIGHT

PREDICTIVE TECHNIQUES

I have not gone into predictive techniques in detail in this book because there just isn't the room for everything. However, I do consider this to be a very important aspect of astrology. Predictive astrology is a bit of a misnomer because fate is something which we each make for ourselves. All that one can do is to show the forthcoming trends and point out to the subject where things are going to flow along easily and where they are not. What he then chooses to do with his life is up to him. Hopefully, awareness creates the ability to make reasoned and sensible choices in life.

Many individuals think that their lives are mapped out before their births by some kind of universal force and that 'gifted' people such as astrologers have the key to this map. These subjects sincerely believe that they only have to consult an astrologer, palmist, Tarot card reader or clairvoyant in order to find out exactly when and where such important matters as finding a husband, having a child or winning the pools will take place. Unfortunately this is not so, but hopefully such people can be shown that it can be very helpful to know that a particular phase is coming to an end and the kind of trend which the new one will bring.

Day-for-a-year progression

The most common form of progression is the day-for-a-year progression, also called secondary direction. This is arrived at by adding as many days to the subject's birthday as his length of life in years. Therefore a person born on 2 April who is now 24 years old would need a chart for 26 April. If you use a computer, then just follow the instructions for day-for-a-year progressions. The new set of figures can be made up into a fresh chart, set around the natal chart (it is useful to use a different colour for this) or just looked at in the form of a list and compared to the natal chart. The meanings of the aspects which are formed by the progressed planets can then be checked in a book like *Predictive Astrology* or *Planets in Transit* (see Further Reading, page 157). Any information on transits can be used for progressions as well, because the rules are the same for both. For instance, a transit of Mars to the Sun will bring a burst of energy while a progression will bring the same but it will go on for a longer period of time.

Don't forget that once you have reached the subject's nearest birthday, you will have to make adjustments for the months which have passed since that date. To do this, you move the Moon forward one degree for each month until you reach the desired date of the reading. It is also worth looking at the Sun, Mercury and Venus to see if they need any further adjustment: if they are coming to the end of a particular degree of a sign at the beginning of the year, they will have moved to the next degree as the year progresses.

Solar arc progressions

There is another form of progression which is called solar arc progression. This consists of moving the whole chart forward one degree for each year of life. I find this fairly useful in readings but, like most astrologers, I prefer secondary directions.

Transits

This is simply a matter of looking in the ephemeris to see where the planets are at the time of the reading and setting them against both the natal chart and the progressed one. Once again, the books by Sakoian and Acker or Robert Hand will help you interpret these.

Retrograde planets

Don't forget that planets can pass backwards over a spot as well as forwards. If Mercury, Venus or Mars is retrograde at birth, they may turn direct by progression during the lifetime (and also vice versa). With the slower-moving planets, they may change direction during a lifetime or they may not. Transiting planets will vary in their motion depending upon which year's chart you wish to study. If a planet passes over a particular spot on the chart and then turns retrograde, it will pass over that spot once more as it goes 'backwards' over the place and then one more time as it passes forwards once again. This can bring a prolonged period of change into the subject's life. Basically speaking, a retrograde planet, whether it is natally retrograde, retrograde by progression or a retrograde transit will bring stress to the subject and this is more important if one of the personal planets is affected.

CHAPTER NINE

'THE HARD STUFF'

One day, perhaps, I shall write a book actually called *The Hard Stuff* which would go into all the really difficult astrological concepts and put them into plain language so that their apparent mysteries are laid open for all to see and understand. Firstly, however, I would have to make sure that I understood them all thoroughly *myself*! The problem is that some of the techniques are recently discovered and have come into being since the advent of cheap personal computers. Thus far, these ideas have only been explained by egg-headed geniuses in the kind of terminology which even a competent practical astrologer may find difficult to follow!

I have included this section chiefly to explain the terminology — if you feel ready to incorporate these ideas into your chart making, it is time to progress to other text books and courses.

The nodes

The nodes of the Moon are the points where the Moon crosses the celestial equator on its way around the Earth. The north node is traditionally supposed to suggest our karmic task in the present life while the south node shows what we did in a past one. I suggest that you take a look at a few charts and assess the signs and houses which the nodes occupy and see how this idea matches up. I have come across some astrology books from America which suggest that the north node is in harmony with the public ethos of the time. For example, a Capricorn north node would have been ideal in the 1980s while a Piscean one would have been much more useful in the early 1970s.

Personally I have also discovered that the nodes have some bearing on premises, property and domestic circumstances. Planets which progress or transit the nodes do seem to bring household changes. These often denote quite minor changes such as decorating or refurbishing a home, receiving visitors or leaving the house for a holiday. If other members of the family go away for a while, this tends to show up as a nodal matter too. A planet which is close to a node in the natal chart, especially the Sun or the Moon is supposed to be especially important.

Midpoints

These are the points which are exactly halfway between two planets, a planet and the ascendant, the midheaven, or any other feature on the chart. There are plenty of them, of course, and they are time-consuming to work out by hand. If you have a computer, then ask it to list all the midpoints in your chart in zodiacal order and see if you have a batch of them in any one part of your chart. This will point to personality traits and also to sensitive areas on your chart of which you were hitherto unaware. It may explain a lot! Certain midpoints will stand out as being important. For example, the midpoint between Mercury and Neptune is a health indicator and can be difficult to live with when it is being transited by other planets. Uranus and any other feature can suggest an important friendship. There are plenty of other things to look for but only time will tell you what is important and what isn't. Sometimes when I am doing a chart for a client, I look at the midpoint list to see if there is a particular area of the chart which is emphasized as this can be useful in interpretation.

Exaltation, detriment and fall

Planets are said to be comfortable in their own sign; for example, Venus in Libra or the Sun in Leo. They are also comfortable in their own house, for example, Mercury in the third. There is also a series of ancient placings which confirm positive or negative vibes. For example, a retrograde Mars in a detrimental sign could suggest the danger of sudden death through some kind of accident, whereas a well-placed planet may be extremely helpful. The chart below only covers the planets which were known before the advent of modern astronomy.

Planet	Exaltation	Fall	Detriment
Sun	Aries	Libra	Aquarius
Moon	Taurus	Scorpio	Capricorn
Mercury	Virgo	Pisces	Sagittarius or Pisces
Venus	Pisces	Virgo	Scorpio or Aries
Mars	Capricorn	Cancer	Libra or Taurus
Jupiter	Cancer	Capricorn	Gemini or Virgo
Saturn	Libra	Aries	Cancer or Leo

Arabic parts

The Arabs discovered a system by which the difference between the ascendant and each planet of the then known zodiac was calculated. This new position became a 'part' of some kind. The only one which I use is the 'part of fortune' which is found by taking the difference between the Sun and the ascendant and adding it to the Moon. The Arabs used any number of these parts and they all had a particular characteristic. The Astrocalc computer programme does give the position of the part of fortune, and it is worth a look at the sign and house this occupies to see how you are going to make your fortune. For example, the part of fortune in the 10th house in Libra would suggest that money can be made by working hard in some kind of partnership.

Fixed stars

These are much easier to understand than Arabic parts because they do at least exist! The planets move around the sky a great deal but the stars do not, hence the term 'fixed stars'. There are plenty of them, as you can imagine, but they each have their characteristics. They can add quite a bit of interest to a chart but, as with the midpoints, you will have to be selective about their use.

Here are a few fixed stars and interpretations which I have taken from the list in Nicholas Campion's *Practical Astrologer*.

Star	Position	Meaning
Algol	26° 6' Taurus	Problems caused by carelessness.
Alcyone	29° 51' Taurus	Emotion, self pity.
Aldaberan	9° 35' Gemini	Confidence, energy, leadership qualities.
Regulus	29° 37' Leo	Pride, good fortune, success.
Vindemiatrix	9° 46' Libra	Self-denial, martyrdom, perhaps for mystical motives.
Spica	23° 38' Libra	Success, prosperity.
Antares	9° 38' Sagittarius	Self-confidence, self-assertion.
Vega	15° 07' Capricorn	Good fortune in worldly ambitions.
Formalhaut	3° 29' Pisces	Beneficial if aspected to Sun, Venus or Jupiter.
Scheat	28° 58' Pisces	Problematical.

Mundane astrology

This term is applied to the astrology of nations, towns and places. The birthchart is taken from the birth of the current administration of these places. The best sources of information on this subject are *Mundane Astrology* and *The Book of World Horoscopes* (see Further Reading). For predictions about Great Britain, you should use the 1801 chart for the 'birth' of the United Kingdom in its present form.

Horary astrology

This is a form of astrology in which a question is asked and the chart has to be made up for the *time* of asking. This is not as straightforward as it sounds because true horary astrology uses techniques which are quite different from those used in normal predictive work.

Electional astrology

This is very useful as it provides a means of choosing the right time to begin an enterprise. The astrologer looks at the ephemeris and tries, within whatever time limit is allowed, to choose the best time to start an activity. The chart then becomes the birthchart of the enterprise. This is used extensively in the Orient for important events such as marriages and business ventures.

There are quite a number of subjects which I have not been able to cover in this section, including harmonics, sidereal Indian astrology, astro-cartography, medical astrology and more, but these tend to be even more involved and not worth tackling until you are totally *au fait* with the techniques in this book. Who knows, perhaps they will be covered in the Hard Stuff book when I get around to writing it!

APPENDIX ONE

SUMMER TIME IN GREAT BRITAIN

As British Summer Time has had a somewhat irregular schedule over the years, here is a table of the time conversions to date. In some years, you will see that there was *Double* Summer Time, where there was an additional one hour's difference from GMT (i.e. two hour's change). In these years, 'Summer' Time actually lasted all year!

All changes are at 2 a.m.

1916	21 MAY — 1 OCT	1924	13 APR — 21 SEPT
1917	8 APR — 17 SEPT	1925	19 APR — 4 OCT
1918	24 MAR — 30 SEPT	1926	18 APR — 3 OCT
1919	30 MAR — 29 SEPT	1927	10 APR — 2 OCT
1920	28 MAR — 25 OCT	1928	22 APR — 7 OCT
1921	3 APR — 3 OCT	1929	21 APR — 6 OCT
1922	26 MAR — 8 OCT	1930	13 APR — 5 OCT
1923	22 APR — 16 SEPT	1931	19 APR — 4 OCT

1932	17 APR — 2 OCT
1933	9 APR — 8 OCT
1934	22 APR — 7 OCT
1935	14 APR — 6 OCT
1936	19 APR — 4 OCT
1937	18 APR — 3 OCT
1938	10 APR — 2 OCT
1939	16 APR — 19 NOV

151

Year	Period	Year	Period	Year	Period
1940	25 FEB — 31 DEC	1954	11 APR — 3 OCT	1974	17 MAR — 27 OCT
1941	1 JAN — 31 DEC	1955	17 APR — 2 OCT	1975	16 MAR — 26 OCT
DST	4 MAY — 10 AUG	1956	22 APR — 7 OCT	1976	21 MAR — 24OCT
1942	1 JAN — 31 DEC	1957	14 APR — 6 OCT	1977	20 MAR — 23 OCT
DST	5 APR — 9 AUG	1958	20 APR — 5 OCT	1978	19 MAR — 29 OCT
1943	1 JAN — 31 DEC	1959	19 APR — 4 OCT	1979	18 MAR — 28 OCT
DST	4 APR — 15 AUG	1960	10 APR — 2 OCT	1980	16 MAR — 26 OCT
1944	1 JAN — 31 DEC	1961	26 MAR — 29 OCT	1981	29 MAR — 25 OCT
DST	2 APR — 17 SEP	1962	25 MAR — 28 OCT	1982	28 MAR — 24 OCT
1945	1 JAN — 7 OCT	1963	31 MAR — 27 OCT	1983	27 MAR — 23 OCT
DST	2 APR — 15 JUL	1964	22 MAR — 25 OCT	1984	25 MAR — 28 OCT
1946	14 APR — 6 OCT	1965	21 MAR — 24 OCT	1985	31 MAR — 27 OCT
1947	16 MAR — 2 NOV	1966	20 MAR — 23 OCT	1986	30 MAR — 26 OCT
DST	13 APR — 10 AUG	1967	19 MAR — 29 OCT	1987	29 MAR — 25 OCT
1948	14 MAR — 31 OCT	1968	18 FEB — 31 DEC	1988	27 MAR — 23 OCT
1949	3 APR — 30 OCT	1969	1 JAN — 31 DEC	1989	26 MAR — 29 OCT
1950	16 APR — 22 OCT	1970	1 JAN — 31 DEC	1990	25 MAR — 28 OCT
1951	15 APR — 21OCT	1971	1 JAN — 31 OCT	1991	
1952	20 APR — 26 OCT	1972	19 MAR — 29 OCT	1992	
1953	19 APR — 4 OCT	1973	18 MAR — 28 OCT	1993	

APPENDIX TWO

SUN SIGN CHANGES

This table shows the time and day in each month when the Sun changes signs. The year is given in the left hand column, and the months are written across the top. For each month the day is given on the left and the time that the Sun is entering the sign on the right. The time is given in GMT. For example, in January 1960 the Sun entered Aquarius(≈) on the 21st day of the month at 1.10 hours (1.10 a.m.).

YEAR	JAN ≈	FEB ✕	MAR ♈	APR ♉	MAY ✕	JUN ♋	JUL ♌	AUG ♍	SEP ♎	OCT ♏	NOV ♐	DEC ♑
1930	20 18.33	19 9.00	21 8.30	20 20.06	21 19.42	22 3.53	23 14.42	23 21.26	23 18.36	24 3.26	23 0.34	22 13.39
1931	21 0.17	19 14.40	21 14.06	21 1.40	22 1.15	22 9.28	23 20.21	24 3.10	24 0.23	24 9.15	23 6.25	22 19.30
1932	21 6.07	19 20.28	20 19.54	20 7.28	21 7.07	21 15.23	23 2.18	23 9.06	23 6.16	23 15.04	22 12.10	22 1.14
1933	20 11.53	19 2.16	21 1.43	20 13.18	21 12.57	21 21.12	23 8.05	23 14.52	23 12.01	23 20.48	22 17.53	22 6.57
1934	20 17.37	19 8.02	21 7.28	21 19.00	21 18.35	22 2.48	23 13.42	23 20.32	23 17.45	24 2.36	22 23.44	22 12.49
1935	20 23.28	19 13.52	21 13.18	21 0.50	22 0.25	22 8.38	23 19.33	23 2.24	23 23.38	24 8.29	23 5.35	22 18.37
1936	21 5.12	19 19.33	20 18.58	20 6.31	21 6.07	21 14.22	23 1.18	23 8.10	23 5.26	23 14.18	22 11.25	22 0.27
1937	20 11.01	19 1.21	21 0.45	20 12.19	21 11.57	21 20.12	23 7.07	23 13.58	23 11.13	23 20.06	22 17.16	22 6.22

YEAR	JAN ♒	FEB ♓	MAR ♈	APR ♉	MAY ♊	JUN ♋	JUL ♌	AUG ♍	SEP ♎	OCT ♏	NOV ♐	DEC ♑
1938	20 16.59	19 7.20	21 6.43	20 18.15	21 17.50	22 2.04	23 12.57	23 19.46	23 16.59	24 1.54	22 23.06	22 12.13
1939	20 22.51	19 13.09	21 12.28	20 23.55	21 23.27	22 7.39	23 18.37	24 1.31	23 22.49	23 7.46	23 4.58	22 18.06
1940	21 4.44	19 19.04	20 18.24	20 5.51	21 5.23	21 13.36	23 0.34	23 7.26	23 4.46	23 13.39	22 10.49	21 23.55
1941	20 10.34	19 0.56	21 0.20	20 11.50	21 11.23	21 19.33	23 6.26	23 13.17	23 10.33	23 19.27	22 16.38	22 5.44
1942	20 16.23	19 6.47	21 6.11	20 17.39	21 17.09	22 1.16	23 12.07	23 18.58	23 16.16	24 1.15	22 22.30	22 11.40
1943	20 22.19	19 12.40	21 12.03	20 23.31	21 23.03	22 7.12	23 18.04	24 0.55	23 22.12	24 7.06	23 4.21	22 17.29
1944	20 4.07	19 18.27	20 17.49	20 5.18	21 4.51	21 13.02	22 23.58	23 6.46	23 4.02	23 12.56	22 10.08	21 23.15
1945	20 9.54	19 0.15	20 23.37	20 11.07	21 10.40	21 18.52	23 5.45	23 12.35	23 9.50	23 18.44	22 15.55	22 5.04
1946	20 15.45	19 6.09	21 5.33	20 17.02	21 16.34	22 0.44	23 11.37	23 18.26	23 15.41	24 0.35	23 21.46	22 10.53
1947	20 21.32	19 11.52	21 11.13	20 22.39	21 22.09	22 6.19	23 17.14	24 0.09	23 21.29	24 6.26	23 3.38	22 16.43
1948	21 3.18	19 17.37	20 16.57	20 4.25	21 3.58	21 12.11	22 23.06	23 6.03	23 3.22	23 12.18	22 9.29	21 22.33
1949	20 9.09	18 23.37	20 22.48	20 10.17	21 9.51	21 18.03	23 4.57	23 11.48	23 9.06	23 18.03	22 15.16	22 4.23
1950	20 15.00	19 5.18	21 4.35	20 15.59	21 15.27	21 23.36	23 10.30	23 17.23	23 14.44	23 23.45	22 21.03	22 10.13
1951	20 20.52	19 11.10	21 10.26	20 21.48	21 21.15	22 5.25	23 16.21	23 23.16	23 20.37	24 5.36	23 2.51	22 16.00
1952	21 2.38	19 16.57	20 16.14	20 3.37	21 3.04	21 11.13	23 22.07	23 5.03	23 2.24	23 11.22	22 8.36	21 21.43
1953	20 8.21	18 22.41	21 22.01	20 9.25	21 8.53	21 17.00	23 3.52	23 10.45	23 8.06	23 17.06	22 14.22	22 3.31
1954	20 14.11	19 4.32	21 3.53	20 15.20	21 14.47	21 22.54	23 9.45	23 16.36	23 13.55	23 22.56	22 20.14	22 9.24
1955	20 20.02	19 10.19	21 9.35	20 20.58	21 20.24	22 4.31	23 15.25	23 22.19	23 19.41	24 4.43	23 2.01	22 15.11
1956	21 1.48	19 16.05	20 15.20	20 2.43	21 2.13	21 10.24	22 21.20	23 4.15	23 1.35	23 10.34	22 7.50	21 21.00
1957	20 7.39	18 21.58	20 21.17	20 8.41	21 8.10	21 16.21	23 3.15	23 10.08	23 7.26	23 16.24	22 13.39	22 2.49
1958	20 13.29	19 3.49	21 3.06	20 14.27	21 13.51	21 21.57	23 8.51	23 15.46	23 13.09	23 22.11	22 19.29	22 8.40
1959	20 19.19	19 9.38	21 8.55	20 20.17	21 19.42	22 3.50	23 14.48	23 21.44	23 19.09	24 4.11	22 1.27	22 14.34
1960	21 1.10	19 15.26	20 14.43	20 2.06	21 1.34	21 9.42	23 20.28	23 3.34	23 0.59	23 10.02	22 7.18	21 20.26
1961	20 7.01	18 21.17	20 20.32	20 7.55	21 7.22	21 15.30	23 2.24	23 9.19	23 6.43	23 15.47	22 13.06	22 2.20
1962	20 12.58	19 3.15	21 2.30	20 13.51	21 13.17	21 21.24	23 8.18	23 15.13	23 12.35	23 21.40	22 19.02	22 8.15
1963	20 18.54	19 9.09	21 8.20	20 19.36	21 18.58	22 3.04	23 13.59	23 20.58	23 18.24	24 3.29	22 0.49	22 14.02
1964	21 0.41	19 14.57	20 14.10	20 1.27	21 0.50	21 8.57	22 19.53	23 2.51	23 0.17	23 9.21	22 6.39	21 19.50
1965	20 6.29	18 20.48	20 20.05	20 7.26	21 6.50	21 14.56	23 1.48	23 8.43	23 6.06	23 15.10	22 12.29	22 1.41
1966	20 12.20	19 2.38	21 1.53	20 13.12	21 12.32	21 20.34	23 7.23	23 14.18	23 11.43	23 20.51	22 18.14	22 7.28

SUN SIGN CHANGES

YEAR	JAN ≈	FEB ⓧ	MAR ♈	APR ♉	MAY Ⅱ	JUN ♋	JUL ♌	AUG ♍	SEP ♎	OCT ♏	NOV ♐	DEC ♑
1967	20 18.08	19 8.24	21 7.37	20 18.55	21 18.18	22 2.23	23 13.16	23 20.13	23 17.38	24 2.44	23 0.05	22 13.16
1968	20 23.54	19 14.09	20 13.22	20 0.41	21 0.06	21 8.13	22 19.06	23 2.03	22 23.26	23 8.30	22 5.49	21 19.00
1969	20 5.38	18 19.55	20 19.06	20 6.27	21 5.50	21 13.55	23 0.48	23 7.44	23 5.07	23 14.11	22 11.31	22 0.44
1970	20 11.24	19 1.42	21 0.57	20 12.15	21 11.38	21 19.43	23 6.37	23 13.34	23 10.59	23 20.04	22 17.35	22 6.36
1971	20 17.13	19 7.27	21 6.38	20 17.54	21 17.15	22 1.20	23 12.15	23 19.15	23 16.45	24 1.53	22 23.14	22 12.24
1972	20 22.59	19 13.12	20 12.22	19 23.38	20 23.00	21 7.06	22 18.03	23 1.03	22 22.33	23 7.42	22 5.03	21 18.13
1973	20 4.48	19 19.01	20 18.13	20 5.31	21 4.54	21 13.01	22 23.56	23 6.54	23 4.21	23 13.30	22 10.54	22 0.06
1974	20 10.46	19 0.59	21 0.07	20 11.19	21 10.36	21 18.38	23 5.30	23 12.29	23 9.59	23 19.11	22 16.39	22 5.56
1975	20 16.37	19 6.50	21 5.57	20 17.06	21 16.24	22 0.27	23 11.22	23 18.24	23 15.55	24 1.06	22 22.31	22 11.46
1976	20 22.25	19 12.40	20 11.50	19 23.03	20 22.21	21 6.25	22 17.19	23 0.19	22 21.48	23 6.58	22 4.22	21 17.35
1977	20 4.15	18 18.31	20 17.43	20 4.58	21 4.15	21 12.14	23 23.04	23 6.01	23 3.30	23 12.41	22 10.07	21 23.23
1978	20 10.04	19 0.21	20 23.34	20 10.50	21 10.09	21 18.10	23 5.01	23 11.57	23 9.26	23 18.37	22 16.05	22 5.21
1979	20 16.00	19 6.14	21 5.22	20 16.36	21 15.54	21 23.57	23 10.49	23 17.47	23 15.17	24 0.28	22 21.54	22 11.10
1980	20 21.49	19 12.02	20 11.10	19 22.23	20 21.42	21 5.47	22 16.42	22 23.41	22 21.09	23 6.18	22 3.42	21 16.56
1981	20 3.36	18 17.52	20 17.03	20 4.19	21 3.40	21 11.45	22 22.40	23 5.39	23 3.06	23 12.13	22 9.36	21 22.51
1982	20 9.31	18 23.47	20 22.56	20 10.08	21 9.23	21 17.23	23 4.16	23 11.16	23 8.47	23 17.58	22 15.24	22 4.39
1983	20 15.17	19 5.31	21 4.39	20 15.51	21 15.07	21 23.09	23 10.05	23 17.08	23 14.42	23 23.55	22 21.19	22 10.30
1984	20 21.05	19 11.17	20 10.25	19 21.39	20 20.58	21 5.03	22 15.59	22 23.01	22 20.33	23 5.46	22 3.11	21 16.23
1985	20 2.58	18 17.08	20 16.14	20 3.26	21 2.43	21 10.45	22 21.37	23 4.36	23 2.06	23 11.22	22 8.51	21 22.08
1986	20 8.47	18 22.58	20 22.03	20 9.13	21 8.28	21 16.30	23 3.25	23 10.26	23 7.59	23 17.15	22 14.45	22 4.03
1987	20 14.41	19 4.50	21 3.52	20 14.58	21 14.10	21 22.11	23 9.06	23 16.10	23 13.46	23 23.01	22 20.30	22 9.46
1988	20 20.25	19 10.36	20 9.39	19 20.45	20 19.57	21 3.57	22 14.52	22 21.54	22 19.29	23 4.45	22 2.12	21 15.28
1989	20 2.07	18 16.21	20 15.29	20 2.39	21 1.54	21 9.53	22 20.46	23 3.47	23 1.20	23 10.36	22 8.05	21 21.22
1990	20 8.02	18 22.14	20 21.20	20 8.27	21 7.38	21 15.33	23 2.22	23 9.21	23 6.56	23 16.14	22 13.47	22 3.07
1991	20 13.48	19 3.59	21 3.02	20 14.09	21 13.21	21 21.19	23 8.12	23 15.13	23 12.49	23 22.06	22 19.36	22 8.54
1992	20 19.33	19 9.44	20 8.49	19 19.57	20 19.13	21 3.15	22 14.09	22 21.11	22 18.43	23 3.58	22 1.26	21 14.44
1993	20 1.23	18 15.36	20 14.41	20 1.50	21 1.02	21 9.00	22 19.51	23 2.51	23 0.23	23 9.38	22 7.07	21 20.26

Time zones around the world

FURTHER READING

John & Peter Filbey, *The Astrologer's Companion* (The Aquarian Press, 1986).
This book goes over everything I have covered here but in greater depth and also far more detail than I have been able to cover. It presents the whole subject in alphabetical order and is a highly recommended reference book.

Derek & Julia Parker, *The New Compleat Astrologer* (Mitchell Beazley, 1984).
A new updated edition of their successful *Compleat Astrologer*, this is a very comprehensive and well presented book for all levels of learning.

Nicholas Campion, *The Practical Astrologer* (Hamlyn, 1987).
Also very comprehensive and highly readable, a book for both beginners and more advanced astrologers alike.

Sasha Fenton, *Moon Signs* (The Aquarian Press, 1987); *Rising Signs* (The Aquarian Press, 1989).
My first two astrology books, they provide all the information you will need about the relevance of the Moon and the ascendant in chart interpretation.

Michael Baigent, Nicholas Campion & Charles Harvey, *Mundane Astrology* (The Aquarian Press, 1984);

Nicholas Campion, *The Book of World Horoscopes* (The Aquarian Press, 1988).

These two books are important for understanding and using the astrology of nations, places and things. The first book is an exhaustive introduction to the subject, and the second is a sourcebook of over 350 charts.

Frances Sakoian & Louis Acker, *Predictive Astrology* (Harper & Row, 1978); *The Astrologer's Handbook* (Penguin Books, 1981).

The first can be used to interpret any kind of progression or transit, and the second gives an excellent interpretation of the planets and the aspects. Two useful and interesting books to have.

Robert Hand, *Planets in Transit* (Para Research, 1976).

Big, easy to read. The most comprehensive book on transits.

Ann Henning, *Modern Astrology* (Robert Hale, 1985).

A good general book which has some interesting ideas and some good exercises to work on.

Sue Tompkins, *Astrological Aspects* (Element Books, 1989).

A truly wonderful book which concentrates on aspects.

Ronald C. Davison, *The Technique of Prediction* (L. N. Fowler, 1956); *Cycles of Destiny* (The Aquarian Press, 1990).

Quite simply the best books on predictive techniques.

Janis Huntley, *Elements of Astrology* (Element Books, 1990).

A good basic book for beginners, if a little stilted and old fashioned in its approach.

Marion March & Joan McEvers, *The Only Way to Learn Astrology* (AstroComputing Services, 1980, 1981, 1983).

An absolutely brilliant set of three books which teach everything you would ever need to know about astrology.

INDEX